D0342060

Are You CHICKEN in the Kitchen?

112 Recipes for Boneless, Skinless Chicken Breasts

Printed in the United States of America
by G&R Publishing Co.

Published By:

507 Industrial Street
Waverly, IA 50677

ISBN-13: 978-1-56383-304-5
ISBN-10: 1-56383-304-2
Item #7031

Table of Contents

With the help of this cookbook, you can whip up 112 delicious family meals. All you'll need is your always-on-hand ingredient: boneless, skinless chicken breast halves.

Chicken Out
Your Dinner:

The Basics of Chicken

Boneless, skinless chicken breast halves are a great staple for any meal. They're quick- and easy-to make, economical and, most of all, tasty! Before you begin preparing your chicken dish, read through these basics about chicken and discover how to get the most out of your meat.

Purchasing Chicken:

At your grocery store, chicken comes in various packaging and forms, including fresh, frozen and canned. It can come whole, breaded, seasoned or even pre-cooked and sliced. All of the recipes in this cookbook call for boneless, skinless chicken breast halves. However, almost all of the recipes could be prepared using whole chicken breasts, chicken parts or chicken breasts with skin. Buying a whole chicken and cutting it into parts is often the cheapest way to purchase chicken. However, buying boneless, skinless chicken will save you a lot of time and effort in the preparation of your meals. Also, white breast meat is low in calories, readily available, and a delicious, juicy part of the chicken. Boneless, skinless chicken breast halves usually come two to four per package in the refrigerated section, with frozen packages containing six to twelve individually frozen chicken breasts or breast halves.

Freezing Chicken:

- If you cannot use purchased fresh chicken within two days, it should be frozen.
- Chicken can be frozen in its original packaging or repackaged.
- If you're planning to freeze chicken for longer than two months, leave the poultry in its original packaging and wrap with heavy-duty aluminum foil or place in a freezer bag.
- Uncooked whole chickens should retain their best flavor and texture for up to one year when wrapped properly and frozen at 0°F or below. Frozen uncooked chicken parts will maintain their best flavor in the same conditions for up to nine months. Never freeze stuffed poultry.

Thawing Chicken:

- Never thaw chicken on your kitchen countertop. Bacteria that can cause food poisoning multiplies rapidly at room temperature.
- The best way to thaw chicken is to place it on a rimmed tray in the refrigerator. Plan on thawing this way for one day per every 5 pounds of chicken, not counting the day you will be preparing the chicken.
- Another safe way to thaw chicken is in cold water. Place chicken in leak-proof wrapping, then place in a sink or large bowl of cold water. Allow 30 minutes of thawing time for every pound of poultry, changing the water every 30 minutes. Cook the thawed chicken as soon as possible.
- Frozen chicken can also be thawed in the microwave.

Place chicken on a microwave-safe rimmed plate and defrost according to microwave instructions based on weight and thickness of chicken. Chicken defrosted in the microwave should be cooked immediately after thawing because some areas of the food may become warm and begin to cook during microwaving.

- Foods defrosted in the microwave or by the cold water method should be cooked before refreezing.

Cooking Chicken:

- Chicken should not be cooked until after it is completely thawed. A partially or completely frozen chicken breast half will not cook evenly. While the outside may look done, the center may not be cooked through.
- Cook chicken to an interior temperature of 165°F in order to kill bacteria.*
- Wash your hands thoroughly before and after handling raw chicken.
- To avoid cross contamination, once raw chicken is transferred to a skillet, grill or baking dish, wash the original plate it was resting on before placing the chicken back on it, or use a different clean plate.
- Another good practice to avoid cross contamination is to use the same cutting board for chicken each time you cook. Use a separate cutting board to prepare vegetables or other foods. Wash cutting boards and utensils thoroughly after each use with hot soapy water, and clean any kitchen surfaces with a disinfectant spray.
- Chicken can be chopped before or after it has been cooked. If chopping chicken before it is cooked, try to

cut pieces of similar size and thickness to ensure even cooking. It is often easier to cut uncooked chicken with kitchen shears. Wash the shears thoroughly with hot soapy water after contact with raw chicken.

* According to the United States Department of Agriculture, bacteria are everywhere in our environment and any food of animal origin can harbor bacteria such as Salmonella or E. coli.

These bacteria can multiply rapidly between the temperatures of 40° to 140°F. To keep these levels low, chicken should be stored in the refrigerator at 40° or less. To destroy the bacteria, chicken should be cooked to at least 165°F.

To Boil Chicken:

The quickest way to cook chicken is to boil it in a pot of hot water. Boiling chicken results in unflavored, bland meat, but it is an ideal method for cooking chicken to be used in salads or soups.

Bring 3 cups of water to a boil in a large pot over medium-high heat. Add two chicken breast halves to the boiling water and cook for 10 to 15 minutes, keeping the temperature high but watching carefully so the pot does not boil over. Remove the chicken from the water and cut a slit in the chicken in order to make sure the center is cooked through and no longer pink inside. Chop or shred as needed. In addition, the boiled liquid can be used as a substitute for chicken broth in recipes.

CHICKEN

Cubed, Sliced & Shredded

Chicken and Tomato Bruschetta

Makes 4 to 6 servings

2 boneless, skinless chicken breast halves
1¼ C. Italian salad dressing, divided
4 C. torn fresh spinach
⅓ C. crumbled feta cheese
8 sun-dried tomatoes, drained and chopped
1 (1 lb.) loaf focaccia bread, cut into ½" slices
¼ C. extra-virgin olive oil

Combine chicken breast halves and 1 cup dressing in a bowl; cover and chill in the refrigerator to marinate for 3 hours. When ready to cook, preheat an outdoor grill to high heat and lightly oil the grate. Discard marinade and grill chicken for 7 minutes per side or until chicken is cooked through and the juices run clear. Set aside the chicken to cool, then shred. In a large bowl, combine shredded chicken, spinach, feta cheese, tomatoes and remaining ¼ cup dressing; set aside. Brush the foccacia slices with olive oil and grill or broil for 1 minute per side or until lightly toasted. Top each toasted slice with a heaping portion of the chicken mixture; serve immediately.

Tropical Chicken Bacon Bites

Makes 8 to 10 servings

4 boneless, skinless chicken breast halves
½ lb. bacon slices
1 (20 oz.) can pineapple chunks, drained
2 C. teriyaki sauce

Chop chicken into bite-size pieces. Cut each bacon slice into thirds. Wrap a small bacon piece around each chicken piece and thread onto a toothpick or small skewer. Thread one pineapple chunk onto each toothpick, next to the chicken. Place skewers on a small rimmed baking sheet; pour teriyaki sauce over top and chill in the refrigerator to marinate for 4 hours. When ready to cook, preheat oven to 375°. Discard the marinade and place skewers on parchment-lined baking sheets; bake for 20 minutes or until chicken is cooked through and the bacon is browned. Drain appetizers on paper towels; serve hot.

Chicken Salad with Cashews and Grapes

Makes 4 servings

2 boneless, skinless chicken breast halves,
   cooked and chopped
1½ C. plain yogurt
¼ C. cole slaw dressing
1 stalk celery, chopped
½ C. chopped sweet onion
Salt and pepper to taste
½ C. quartered grapes
½ C. chopped cashews

In a food processor, combine cooked chicken, yogurt, dressing, celery, onion, salt and pepper; pulse until coarsely chopped. In a medium bowl, combine the salad mixture with grapes and cashews; stir well. Serve immediately or spread over slices of bread to make sandwiches.

Asian Chicken Salad

Makes 6 servings

1 pkg. Oriental-flavored Ramen noodles
4 boneless, skinless chicken breast halves,
  cooked and chopped
2 heads Napa cabbage, shredded
1 (11 oz.) can mandarin oranges, drained
1 bunch green onions, chopped
2 to 3 T. shelled sunflower seeds
2 to 3 T. slivered almonds
2 to 3 T. cashew halves and pieces
1 C. vegetable oil
½ C. red wine vinegar
1 T. soy sauce
½ C. sugar

Preheat oven to 350°. Break up Ramen noodles and spread out on a baking sheet; sprinkle with seasoning packet. Bake noodles for 5 minutes or until lightly toasted; set aside to cool. In a large bowl, combine chicken, cabbage, oranges, green onions, sunflower seeds, almonds and cashews. In a medium bowl, whisk together oil, vinegar, soy sauce and sugar. Pour dressing over chicken mixture; add noodles and toss until evenly incorporated. Serve salad immediately.

Orange Vinaigrette Chicken Salad

Makes 4 servings

½ C. orange juice
½ C. white wine vinegar
¼ C. extra-virgin olive oil
¼ C. garlic and herb seasoning blend
1½ T. sugar
4 boneless, skinless chicken breast halves
1 head romaine lettuce, chopped
1 (11 oz.) can mandarin oranges, drained
1 C. chopped fresh broccoli
1 C. chopped baby carrots

Preheat an outdoor grill to medium-high heat and lightly oil the grate. In a medium bowl, combine orange juice, vinegar, olive oil, seasoning blend and sugar; mix well and set aside ½ cup for basting. Grill chicken for 6 to 8 minutes per side or until chicken is cooked through and the juices run clear, basting frequently with the reserved sauce. Set aside the chicken to cool, then cut into strips. Discard any remaining sauce used for basting. In a large bowl, toss together lettuce, oranges, broccoli and carrots; top with the chicken strips and drizzle with remaining sauce. Serve immediately.

Rotini Chicken Salad

4 boneless, skinless chicken breast halves
Steak seasoning
8 oz. uncooked rotini pasta
8 oz. mozzarella cheese, cubed
1 red onion, chopped
1 head romaine lettuce, chopped
6 cherry tomatoes, chopped

Preheat an outdoor grill to medium-high heat and lightly oil the grate. Season chicken with desired amount of steak seasoning. Grill chicken for 6 to 8 minutes per side or until chicken is cooked through and the juices run clear. Set aside the chicken to cool, then cut into strips. Meanwhile, cook pasta in a large pot of lightly salted boiling water for 8 to 10 minutes or until al dente; drain and rinse with cool water. In a large bowl, combine cheese, onion, lettuce and tomatoes. Add chicken and pasta to ingredients in bowl; toss until well combined and serve immediately.

Chicken Fiesta Salad

Makes 4 servings

4 (6") corn tortillas
Vegetable oil for frying
1 head leafy lettuce, torn
1 large yellow bell pepper,
cut into thin strips
1 large mango, peeled,
seeded and cubed
1 large avocado, peeled,
pitted and sliced
2 plum tomatoes,
finely chopped
1 (15 oz.) can black beans,
rinsed and drained
1 C. shredded Pepper Jack cheese

4 boneless, skinless chicken
breast halves
1 (1.25 oz.) pkg. taco
seasoning
1 tsp. chili powder
2 T. water
⅓ C. vegetable oil
⅓ C. lime juice
2 T. honey
⅓ C. chopped fresh cilantro
2 tsp. Dijon mustard

In a large nonstick skillet, heat a small amount of oil over medium heat. Cut corn tortillas into ¼" strips; fry in hot oil for 1 to 2 minutes or until golden and crisp. Set strips on paper towels to drain. On four dinner plates, layer an even amount of lettuce, bell pepper strips, mango, avocado, tomatoes, black beans and cheese. Cook chicken in same skillet over medium heat for 4 to 6 minutes per side or until chicken is cooked through and the juices run clear. Sprinkle chicken with taco seasoning, chili powder and water during cooking time. Remove chicken from skillet and cut into ¼" strips. In a food processor, combine ⅓ cup vegetable oil, lime juice, honey, cilantro and mustard; pulse until well combined. Place cooked chicken strips over each salad and drizzle each with about 3 tablespoons of the dressing mixture; top with tortilla strips.

Mediterranean Chicken Salad

Makes 4 servings

½ C. plain yogurt
¼ C. mayonnaise or creamy salad dressing
2 or 3 boneless, skinless chicken breast halves,
   cooked and diced
½ C. crumbled feta cheese
¼ C. diced, seeded cucumber
¼ C. chopped, pitted Kalamata olives
2 T. sliced green onions
½ tsp. grated lemon peel
2 plum tomatoes, seeded and diced

In a medium bowl, combine yogurt and mayonnaise, mixing until smooth. Stir in diced chicken, cheese, cucumber, olives, green onions, lemon peel and tomatoes; toss until well combined. Serve immediately or spread over slices of bread to make sandwiches.

Smokin' Sweet Chicken Wraps

Makes 8 servings

½ C. mayonnaise or creamy salad dressing
¼ C. diced, seeded cucumber
2 tsp. Spanish smoked sweet paprika, divided
½ tsp. pepper
2 T. honey, divided
2 tsp. extra-virgin olive oil
6 boneless, skinless chicken breast halves, cut into strips
1 C. chunky salsa
8 (8") flour tortillas
8 large lettuce leaves

In a small bowl, combine mayonnaise, cucumber, 1 teaspoon paprika, pepper and 1 tablespoon honey; cover and set aside in refrigerator. Heat oil in a large nonstick skillet over medium-high heat. Add chicken strips and cook for 5 to 8 minutes or until chicken is cooked through and no longer pink, stirring frequently. Stir in salsa, remaining 1 teaspoon paprika and remaining 1 tablespoon honey. Reduce heat to medium-low and simmer, uncovered, for 5 minutes, stirring occasionally. If desired, stir in an additional 1 to 2 teaspoons paprika. Wrap tortillas in damp paper towels and microwave for 10 to 20 seconds or until warm and pliable. Spread 1 tablespoon mayonnaise mixture over each tortilla; top each with 1 large lettuce leaf and about ½ cup of the chicken mixture. Fold tortillas to make wraps; serve immediately.

Easy Chicken Enchiladas

Makes 4 to 6 servings

1 (10.7 oz.) can cream of chicken soup
½ C. milk
½ C. sour cream
1 (4 oz.) can diced green chiles, drained
4 boneless, skinless chicken breast halves,
   cooked and chopped
¼ C. chopped fresh cilantro
½ C. salsa
Pinch of ground cumin
6 (6") corn or flour tortillas
1 C. shredded Cheddar cheese

Preheat oven to 325°. In a medium bowl, combine soup, milk, sour cream and chiles; mix well. In a separate bowl, toss together cooked chicken, cilantro, salsa and cumin; add 2 tablespoons of the sauce mixture and mix well. Spread ½ cup of the sauce mixture over the bottom of a lightly greased 9 x 13" baking dish. Divide meat mixture evenly and place on tortillas. Roll tortillas and place, seam side down, in the baking dish. Pour remaining sauce evenly over rolled tortillas and top with cheese. Cover dish with aluminum foil; bake for 30 minutes.

Dijon Chicken Casserole

Makes 4 to 6 servings

6 boneless, skinless chicken breast halves, chopped
¼ C. Italian salad dressing
1 tsp. dried thyme
Salt and pepper to taste
2 C. frozen mixed broccoli, cauliflower
  and carrots, thawed
¼ C. butter, melted
¼ C. flour
2 C. milk
2 T. Dijon mustard
2 C. shredded Cheddar and
  Monterey Jack cheese blend, divided

Preheat oven to 375°. In a large nonstick skillet over medium-high heat, sauté chicken in Italian dressing and thyme until chicken is cooked through and no longer pink; season with salt and pepper to taste. Spread cooked chicken and thawed vegetables in a greased 9 x 13" baking dish. In a medium bowl, combine butter and flour, stirring until a paste forms. Mix in milk and mustard; season to taste with salt and pepper. Heat sauce in microwave for about 3 minutes, or until thickened, stirring after every minute. Stir in 1 cup cheese until melted; pour over ingredients in baking dish. Sprinkle remaining 1 cup cheese over top. Bake for 20 to 30 minutes or until casserole is bubbling hot.

Easy Chicken Dinner Bake

Makes 4 servings

4 boneless, skinless chicken breast halves
1 (8 oz.) can sliced water chestnuts, drained
1 onion, chopped
1 (10.7 oz.) can cream of chicken soup
1 C. crushed corn flake cereal, divided
1 C. mayonnaise

Preheat oven to 350°. In a large pot filled with water, boil chicken until cooked through and no longer pink. Remove chicken from pot and cut into small pieces. In a large bowl, combine chicken, water chestnuts, onion, soup, ¾ cup crushed cereal and mayonnaise; mix until well combined. Spread mixture into a 9 x 13" baking dish. Sprinkle the remaining crushed cereal over top. Bake casserole for 1 hour.

Simple Chicken Pot Pie

Makes 6 to 8 servings

*4 boneless, skinless chicken breast halves,
   cooked and diced*
1 (10.7 oz.) can cream of chicken soup
2 (15 oz.) cans mixed vegetables, drained
1 (15 oz.) box refrigerated 9" pie crusts (2 count)

Preheat oven to 375°. In a medium bowl, combine cooked chicken, soup and mixed vegetables; set aside. Place one pie pastry layer in a 9" pie plate; fill with chicken mixture. Place remaining pie pastry layer over chicken mixture and flute the edges to seal. Poke a few holes in the top pastry for ventilation. Bake for 45 minutes or until crust is golden brown.

Chicken Curry Pizza

Makes 6 servings

1 (13.8 oz.) tube refrigerated
pizza crust
2 T. vegetable oil
2 boneless, skinless chicken
breast halves, diced
1 C. chopped onion
½ C. chopped red bell pepper
2 cloves garlic, minced
½ tsp. salt
¼ tsp. ground coriander
¼ tsp. ground cumin

¼ tsp. ground ginger
⅛ tsp. ground turmeric
⅛ tsp. cayenne pepper
⅛ tsp. ground cinnamon
⅛ tsp. ground cloves
1 C. chopped tomatoes
½ C. frozen sweet peas,
thawed
1 C. shredded mozzarella
cheese

Preheat oven to 350°. Lightly grease a 9 x 13" baking dish or 12" pizza pan. Unroll pizza crust dough and press into baking dish or pizza pan; bake for 15 to 20 minutes or until lightly golden. Heat oil in a large nonstick skillet over medium-high heat. Add chicken, onion, bell pepper, garlic, salt, coriander, cumin, ginger, turmeric, cayenne pepper, cinnamon and cloves; sauté for 6 to 8 minutes or until chicken is cooked through and no longer pink and the onions are tender. Stir in tomatoes and peas; sauté for an additional 3 minutes or until tomatoes are soft. Spread mixture evenly over partially-baked crust; top with cheese. Bake for 17 to 22 minutes or until the edges of crust are golden and the cheese is melted. Remove from oven and let stand for 10 minutes before cutting into slices and serving.

Chicken Asparagus Stir-Fry

Makes 4 servings

4 boneless, skinless chicken breast halves,
  cut into thin strips
2 T. cornstarch, divided
2 T. soy sauce
2 T. oyster sauce
½ tsp. dark sesame oil, optional
3 T. vegetable oil, divided
8 oz. fresh asparagus spears, cut into 2" pieces
1 small red bell pepper, cut into strips
1 medium onion, sliced
1 clove garlic, minced
1 (14 oz.) can chicken broth
1 (8 oz.) can sliced water chestnuts, drained

Toss chicken strips with 1 tablespoon cornstarch in a medium bowl. In a separate bowl, combine remaining 1 tablespoon cornstarch, soy sauce, oyster sauce and sesame oil; set aside. Heat 2 tablespoons vegetable oil in a large nonstick skillet or wok over medium-high heat; add chicken and stir-fry for 5 minutes or until chicken is cooked through and no longer pink. Remove chicken to a plate and keep warm. Heat remaining 1 tablespoon oil in skillet or wok. Add asparagus, bell pepper, onion and garlic to skillet; stir-fry for 1 minute. Add broth to skillet, cover and cook for 4 minutes or until vegetables are tender but crisp. Return chicken to skillet; stir in water chestnuts and cornstarch mixture. Heat for 1 minute or until sauce thickens; serve immediately.

Kiwi Chicken Stir-Fry

Makes 4 servings

¾ C. chicken broth
2 T. soy sauce
1 T. fresh lemon juice
2 tsp. brown sugar
1 tsp. grated lemon peel
1 tsp. balsamic vinegar
¼ tsp. crushed red pepper flakes
4 boneless, skinless chicken breast halves, cubed
2 T. cornstarch
2 T. peanut oil, divided
1 red bell pepper, chopped
6 green onions, cut into 2" pieces
2 T. minced garlic
2 T. minced fresh gingerroot
3 kiwi fruit, peeled and cut into ¼" pieces

In a medium bowl, combine chicken broth, soy sauce, lemon juice, brown sugar, lemon peel, vinegar and red pepper flakes; mix well and set aside. Dredge chicken pieces in cornstarch until evenly coated. Heat 1 tablespoon peanut oil in a large nonstick skillet or wok over medium-high heat; add chicken and stir-fry for 5 minutes or until chicken is cooked through and no longer pink. Remove chicken to a plate and keep warm. Heat remaining 1 tablespoon oil in skillet or wok. Add bell pepper, green onions, garlic and gingerroot; stir-fry for 1 to 2 minutes. Return chicken to wok and stir in broth mixture; heat for 2 minutes. Add kiwi and stir-fry for 1 minute. Serve immediately.

Cashew Chicken Stir-Fry

Makes 4 servings

1 egg white, beaten
1 T. rice wine vinegar
3 or 4 boneless, skinless chicken breast halves, cubed
3 T. vegetable oil, divided
1 C. cashew halves
1 (8 oz.) can sliced water chestnuts, drained
1 (8 oz.) can bamboo shoots, drained
3 stalks celery, thinly sliced
1 small sweet onion, thinly sliced
2 red bell peppers, thinly sliced
½ C. chicken broth
2 T. cornstarch
2 T. soy sauce
2 tsp. dark sesame oil

In a medium bowl, combine egg white and vinegar; stir in chicken pieces and chill in refrigerator for 1 hour to marinate. Heat 1 tablespoon vegetable oil in a large nonstick skillet or wok over medium-high heat; add cashews and stir-fry for 30 seconds. Add remaining 2 tablespoons oil and drained chicken pieces; stir-fry for 5 minutes or until chicken is cooked through and no longer pink. Stir in water chestnuts, bamboo shoots, celery, onion and bell peppers; stir-fry for 3 to 5 minutes or until tender but crisp. In a small bowl, combine chicken broth, cornstarch, soy sauce and sesame oil; pour over ingredients in skillet and heat until sauce thickens. Serve immediately.

Hot Orange Chicken Toss

Makes 4 servings

2 T. extra-virgin olive oil
1 large onion, thinly sliced
4 boneless, skinless chicken breast halves, cubed
1 T. cornstarch
1 tsp. curry powder
½ tsp. salt
½ tsp. ground ginger
½ tsp. ground cumin
2 C. orange juice
1 yellow or orange bell pepper, chopped
1 (8 oz.) can sliced water chestnuts, drained
3 C. fresh broccoli florets
Zest of 1 orange

Preheat a large nonstick skillet over medium-high heat. Add oil and onion; sauté for 2 minutes then stir in chicken pieces. Heat chicken, stirring often, until cooked through and no longer pink. Add cornstarch, curry powder, salt, ginger and cumin. Mix in orange juice and continue to cook until mixture is thickened and bubbly. Stir in bell pepper, water chestnuts and broccoli; cook until tender but crisp. Mix in orange zest, stirring well. Serve immediately.

Chicken Scampi

½ C. butter or margarine
¼ C. extra-virgin olive oil
1 tsp. dried parsley flakes
1 tsp. dried basil
¼ tsp. dried oregano
3 cloves garlic, minced
¾ tsp. salt
1 T. lemon juice
4 boneless, skinless chicken breast halves, chopped

Heat butter and oil in a large nonstick skillet over medium-high heat. Once butter is melted, stir in parsley, basil, oregano, garlic and salt; mix well and stir in lemon juice. Add chicken pieces and sauté for about 3 minutes. Reduce heat to medium-low and simmer, uncovered, for about 10 minutes or until chicken is cooked through and no longer pink. If necessary, stir in more butter. Serve immediately.

Asparagus Chicken over Wild Rice

Makes 4 servings

6 T. hoisin sauce
2 T. brown sugar
4 T. peanut oil, divided
1 lb. fresh asparagus spears, cut into 1" pieces
2 boneless, skinless chicken breast halves, cubed
4 C. prepared wild rice, divided

In a small bowl, combine hoisin sauce and brown sugar; set aside. Preheat a large nonstick skillet or wok over medium-high heat. Once skillet is hot, drizzle 2 tablespoons peanut oil in skillet; add asparagus pieces and stir-fry for 2 minutes. Remove asparagus to a plate and keep warm. Heat wok to high heat then add remaining 2 tablespoons peanut oil and chicken pieces; stir-fry for 5 minutes or until chicken is cooked through and no longer pink. Return asparagus to skillet and stir in hoisin mixture, toss until evenly coated. Place 1 cup prepared wild rice on each of four plates. Spoon hot chicken and asparagus over each serving.

Thai Chicken Skewers

½ C. creamy peanut butter
½ C. water
¼ C. soy sauce
4 cloves garlic, minced
3 T. lemon juice
2 T. brown sugar
¾ tsp. ground ginger
½ tsp. crushed red pepper flakes
4 boneless, skinless chicken breast halves,
   cut into 1" strips
2 C. shredded red cabbage, divided
4 green onions, chopped

Preheat an outdoor grill to medium-high heat and lightly oil the grate. In a large saucepan over medium-high heat, combine peanut butter, water, soy sauce, garlic, lemon juice, brown sugar, ginger and red pepper flakes; heat for 5 minutes, stirring until smooth. Set aside half of the sauce. Thread chicken strips, accordion-style, onto metal or soaked wooden skewers. Grill chicken for 2 minutes. Use remaining sauce for basting; brush over chicken skewers. Turn skewers over and grill for 4 to 6 minutes or until chicken is cooked through and no longer pink, basting often with the sauce. Divide cabbage evenly onto four plates. Place a few chicken skewers over cabbage on each plate; sprinkle with green onions. Serve reserved sauce on the side for dipping.

Chicken Strawberry Kabobs

Makes 4 to 6 servings

1 C. lemon juice
2 (8 oz.) cans pineapple chunks, juice reserved
Salt and pepper to taste
2 tsp. ground cinnamon, divided
3 boneless, skinless chicken breast halves, cubed
1 C. butter, melted
2 T. brown sugar
1 tsp. ground nutmeg
24 large strawberries

In a shallow bowl, combine lemon juice, pineapple juice, salt, pepper and 1 teaspoon cinnamon; add chicken pieces and chill in refrigerator for 1 hour to marinate. When ready to cook, preheat an outdoor grill to medium-high heat and lightly oil the grate. In a small bowl, combine butter, remaining 1 teaspoon cinnamon, brown sugar and nutmeg. Thread drained chicken pieces, pineapple chunks and strawberries onto metal or soaked wooden skewers, using about 4 to 6 pieces for each skewer. Brush kabobs with butter mixture and grill for 4 to 6 minutes on each side or until strawberries are sizzling and chicken is cooked through.

Honey Chicken Kabobs

Makes 4 to 6 servings

2 T. vegetable oil
3 T. honey
3 T. soy sauce
⅛ tsp. pepper
4 boneless, skinless chicken breast halves, cubed
2 cloves garlic
5 small onions, cut into 2" pieces
2 red bell peppers, cut into 2" pieces

In a medium bowl, whisk together oil, honey, soy sauce and pepper; set aside 3 tablespoons of the sauce. Add chicken pieces, garlic, onions and bell peppers to bowl; cover and refrigerate for 2 hours to marinate. When ready to cook, preheat an outdoor grill to medium-high heat and lightly oil the grate. Drain chicken and vegetables, discarding the marinade. Thread chicken and vegetables alternately onto metal or soaked wooden skewers. Grill kabobs for 4 to 6 minutes on each side or until chicken is cooked through, brushing with the reserved sauce.

Individual Chicken Stew Mugs

Makes 8 servings

1 (16.3 oz.) tube jumbo refrigerated biscuits (8 count)
Spanish sweet paprika
6 boneless, skinless chicken breast halves, chopped
3 T. butter or margarine
2 stalks celery, chopped
1 medium yellow onion, chopped
1 large carrot, peeled and diced
Salt and pepper to taste
2 tsp. poultry seasoning
3 T. flour
1 C. frozen shredded hash brown potatoes
1 pint half n' half
4 C. chicken broth
¼ tsp. ground nutmeg
1 C. frozen green peas

Preheat oven to 350°. Place biscuits on a baking sheet. Sprinkle a small amount of paprika over each biscuit, then bake for 14 to 17 minutes or until golden brown. In a large nonstick Dutch oven or saucepan over medium-high heat, cook chicken pieces in butter for 2 minutes. Stir in celery, onion, carrot, salt, pepper and poultry seasoning; heat for 5 minutes, then stir in flour and cook for 1 minute more. Stir in potatoes, then whisk in half n' half, chicken broth and nutmeg. Bring mixture to a boil, then reduce heat and let stew simmer for 10 minutes, making sure chicken is cooked through. Stir in peas and cook until peas are heated through. Ladle mixture evenly into eight mugs. Top each mug with one of the warm biscuits and serve immediately.

Cilantro Lime Chicken Soup

Makes 4 servings

1 T. extra-virgin olive oil
1 medium sweet onion, chopped
1 T. minced garlic
1 (14 oz.) can diced tomatoes with basil,
   garlic and oregano, juice reserved
3 (14 oz.) cans chicken broth
2 boneless, skinless chicken breast halves,
   cooked and shredded
Juice of 1 lime
⅓ C. chopped fresh cilantro
Salt and pepper to taste

Heat oil in a large nonstick skillet over medium-high heat. Add onion and garlic; sauté for 5 minutes. Stir drained tomatoes into skillet and heat for 5 minutes; set aside. Bring chicken broth to a simmer in a large saucepan over medium-high heat. Stir in cooked chicken, lime juice, cilantro, juice from tomatoes, and the sautéed mixture; season with salt and pepper to taste. Reduce heat to low and let soup simmer for 30 minutes, stirring occasionally.

Chicken and Broccoli Cheese Soup

Makes 6 to 8 servings

6 boneless, skinless chicken breast halves
4 C. water
4 C. chopped fresh or frozen broccoli
½ C. chopped sweet onion
½ C. chopped celery
2 cloves garlic, minced
1 (15 oz.) can cream-style corn
1½ C. shredded Cheddar cheese
1 C. half n' half
Salt and pepper to taste
1 C. seasoned croutons, divided

Bring water to a boil in a large saucepan over medium-high heat. Cook chicken breast halves in boiling water until cooked through and no longer pink. Set aside chicken to cool, then cut into small pieces. Add broccoli, onion, celery and garlic to water in saucepan; bring to a boil then reduce heat to medium-low and simmer until vegetables are tender, about 15 minutes. Return cooked chicken to saucepan and stir in corn, cheese and half n' half. Continue to heat until cheese is completely melted. Season soup to taste with salt and pepper. Ladle soup into bowls and top each serving with a few croutons.

Chicken Tortilla Soup

Makes 6 to 8 servings

3 (48 oz.) cans chicken broth
8 boneless, skinless chicken breast halves, cubed
½ C. plus 1 T. extra-virgin olive oil, divided
6 large carrots, thinly sliced
1 red bell pepper, chopped
3 cloves garlic, minced
1 (12 oz.) jar salsa
2 T. ground cumin
1 tsp. salt
1 tsp. pepper
3 T. chopped fresh cilantro
4 (6") corn tortillas
2 T. lime juice
1½ C. shredded Monterey Jack cheese, divided

Heat chicken broth in a large saucepan over medium-high heat. Meanwhile, sauté cubed chicken in ¼ cup oil in a large nonstick skillet over medium-high heat until lightly browned. Add another ¼ cup oil, carrots, bell pepper and garlic to skillet; sauté until vegetables are softened and chicken is cooked through. Drain vegetables and chicken; add to broth in saucepan along with salsa, cumin, salt, pepper and cilantro. Simmer the soup for 10 minutes. In the same skillet, heat remaining 1 tablespoon oil over medium heat. Cut corn tortillas into ¼" strips; fry in hot oil for 1 to 2 minutes or until golden and crisp. Set strips on paper towels to drain and set aside. Stir lime juice into soup. Ladle soup into bowls. Garnish each serving with some tortilla strips and a few tablespoons of shredded cheese.

Chicken and Wild Rice Soup

Makes 6 to 8 servings

10 C. chicken broth, divided
1 C. uncooked wild rice
¼ C. butter
1 large white onion, chopped
2 to 3 cloves garlic, minced
4 stalks celery, diced
2 C. sliced mushrooms
4 medium carrots, peeled and diced
½ C. flour
2 tsp. dried savory, sage or thyme
3 boneless, skinless chicken breast halves,
   cooked and cubed
2 to 3 T. lemon juice
Salt and pepper to taste

Bring 4 cups chicken broth and wild rice to a boil in a large saucepan over medium high heat. Reduce heat to low, cover and simmer for 50 to 60 minutes or until the rice is tender; do not drain. Meanwhile, melt butter in a large nonstick skillet over medium-high heat. Add onion, garlic, celery, mushrooms and carrots to skillet; sauté until vegetables are tender. Stir in flour and savory; continue to heat until slightly thickened and bubbly. Add mixture to wild rice along with chicken and remaining 6 cups chicken broth; simmer over low heat for 30 minutes, making sure chicken is cooked through. Stir in lemon juice and season with salt and pepper just before serving.

White Chicken Chili

Makes 6 servings

1 tsp. extra-virgin olive oil
1 clove garlic, minced
1 medium onion, chopped
1 (15.5 oz.) can Great Northern beans, drained
1½ C. chicken broth
4 boneless, skinless chicken breast halves,
    cooked and shredded
1 (4 oz.) can diced green chiles, drained
1 tsp. ground cumin
¾ tsp. dried oregano
⅛ tsp. ground cloves
⅛ tsp. cayenne pepper
Salt and pepper to taste
1 C. shredded Cheddar or
    Monterey Jack cheese, divided
Salsa and sour cream for garnish

Heat oil in a large saucepan over medium-high heat. Stir in garlic and onion; sauté until tender. Mix in beans and chicken broth. Stir in cooked chicken, chiles, cumin, oregano, cloves and cayenne pepper. Season with salt and pepper to taste. Heat chili over low heat for 30 to 40 minutes. Ladle chili into bowls. Garnish each serving with some of the shredded cheese, salsa and a dollop of sour cream.

Hawaiian Grilled Quesadillas

Makes 4 servings

6 T. extra-virgin olive oil, divided

2 T. apple cider vinegar

1 T. honey

⅓ C. fresh chopped cilantro

2 cloves garlic, minced

¼ tsp. salt

⅛ tsp. pepper

1 C. finely chopped pineapple

½ C. finely chopped kiwi

½ C. finely chopped mango

½ C. minced red onion

4 boneless, skinless chicken breast halves

8 (12") flour tortillas

3 C. shredded Monterey Jack cheese

To make salsa, in a large bowl, whisk together 4 tablespoons oil, vinegar, honey, cilantro, garlic, salt and pepper. Stir in pineapple, kiwi, mango and red onion. Transfer 1 cup of the salsa and all juices from salsa to a large zippered plastic bag. Cover and refrigerate remaining salsa. Add chicken to salsa and juice in bag. Seal bag, removing any air. Shake bag slightly and chill in refrigerator for 30 minutes to 1 hour to marinate. Preheat an outdoor grill to medium-high heat and lightly oil the grate. Grill the chicken, discarding the marinade, for 10 to 12 minutes or until the chicken is cooked through and no longer pink. Let chicken cool, then finely chop. Brush one side of each tortilla with remaining oil. Place four tortillas on grill, oiled side down. Sprinkle half of the cheese over the tortillas. Top each with ¼ of the chopped chicken and reserved salsa. Sprinkle with remaining cheese and top with remaining four tortillas, oiled side up. Grill quesadillas for 1 to 2 minutes per side or until the cheese has melted.

Pesto Chicken Pizza

Makes 4 servings

2 boneless, skinless chicken breast halves
½ C. Italian salad dressing
1 (12") baked pizza crust
6 oz. prepared pesto sauce
1 (4 oz.) can sliced black olives, drained
1½ C. shredded Cheddar cheese

Place chicken in a shallow bowl; pour Italian dressing over top. Cover and chill in the refrigerator for 1 hour to marinate. Preheat an outdoor grill to medium-high heat and lightly oil the grate. Grill the chicken, discarding the marinade, for 10 to 12 minutes or until the chicken is cooked through and no longer pink. Let chicken cool, then cut into thin strips. Preheat oven to 425°. Spread pesto sauce over pizza crust. Top with olives, chicken strips and cheese. Bake for 10 to 12 minutes or until the cheese has melted.

CHICKEN

Sautéed & Fried

Chicken Breast Supreme

Makes 4 servings

4 boneless, skinless chicken breast halves
½ tsp. salt
¼ tsp. pepper
1 T. extra-virgin olive oil
1½ T. butter, divided
3 T. chopped green onions
Juice of ½ lemon
3 T. chopped fresh parsley
2 tsp. Dijon mustard
¼ C. chicken broth

Pound chicken breast halves with a mallet to about ¼" thickness; sprinkle with salt and pepper. Heat oil and 1 tablespoon butter in a large nonstick skillet over high heat. Cook chicken breast halves in oil for about 4 minutes per side or until cooked through. Remove chicken to a plate and keep warm. Add green onions, lemon juice, parsley and mustard to skillet; heat and stir for about 15 seconds. Add chicken broth to skillet and stir until smooth. Remove from heat and stir in remaining ½ tablespoon butter. Place one cooked chicken breast half on each of four serving plates. Spoon a generous amount of the sauce over each serving.

Cheesy Chicken Skillet

Makes 4 servings

4 boneless, skinless chicken breast halves
¼ tsp. garlic pepper seasoning or seasoned salt
1 C. chicken broth
¾ C. water
2 C. frozen broccoli florets
2 C. uncooked instant white rice
¾ C. light Velveeta cheese

Sprinkle chicken breast halves on both sides with garlic pepper seasoning. Heat a large nonstick skillet over medium-high heat and spray with nonstick cooking spray. Add chicken to skillet, cover and cook for 4 minutes per side or until well browned. Remove chicken to a plate and keep warm. Add chicken broth, water and broccoli to same skillet over medium-high heat; bring to a boil. Stir in rice and return to a boil. Place chicken over ingredients in skillet. Cover skillet and reduce heat to low; cook for 5 to 10 minutes or until all of the liquid has been absorbed and chicken is cooked through. Remove chicken to a plate and keep warm. Stir cheese into ingredients in skillet until cheese is completely melted. Place an even portion of the cheesy rice mixture on each of four serving plates; top each with one cooked chicken breast half.

Chicken, Broccoli and Rice Dinner

Makes 4 to 6 servings

2 T. extra-virgin olive oil
1 T. butter
1 onion, chopped
4 boneless, skinless chicken breast halves
1 (8 oz.) pkg. sliced fresh mushrooms
1½ C. water
1 (6 oz.) pkg. chicken-flavored long grain wild rice mix
1 (10 oz.) pkg. frozen chopped broccoli
½ C. sour cream
½ C. grated Parmesan cheese

Heat oil and butter in a large nonstick skillet over medium-high heat; add onion and sauté until tender. Add chicken breast halves to skillet and heat for 4 minutes on one side. Turn chicken over and add mushrooms; heat until chicken is cooked through. Push chicken to sides of skillet. Add water and rice mix with seasoning packet to skillet. Place broccoli in center of skillet; cover and bring mixture to a boil. Reduce the heat to low and continue to cook, covered, for 10 minutes. Stir well and mix in sour cream; heat for 1 to 2 minutes. Sprinkle with Parmesan cheese and heat for 2 minutes or until cheese is melted.

Spiced Chicken with Tomatoes

Makes 4 servings

¾ tsp. chili powder
½ tsp. salt
½ tsp. ground cumin
¼ tsp. garlic powder
⅛ tsp. cayenne pepper
4 boneless, skinless chicken breast halves
1 tsp. vegetable oil
¼ C. chopped green onions
1 jalapeño pepper, seeded and minced
1 clove garlic, minced
1 (14.5 oz.) can diced tomatoes, drained
1 tsp. cornstarch
2 tsp. water

In a small bowl, combine chili powder, salt, cumin, garlic powder and cayenne pepper; rub over both sides of chicken breast halves. Cook chicken in oil in a large nonstick skillet over medium-high heat until lightly browned on both sides. Add onions, jalapeño and garlic to skillet; sauté for 1 minute. Stir in tomatoes and bring to a boil; reduce heat, cover and simmer for 15 to 20 minutes or until chicken is cooked through. Remove chicken to a plate and keep warm. In a small bowl, combine cornstarch and water; stir into tomato mixture. Bring mixture to a boil for 1 minute, stirring constantly, until slightly thickened. Place one cooked chicken breast half on each of four serving plates. Spoon a generous amount of the tomato sauce over each serving.

Colby-Jack Smothered Chicken

Makes 4 servings

4 boneless, skinless chicken breast halves
¼ tsp. salt
¼ tsp. lemon pepper seasoning
1 T. vegetable oil
8 strips bacon
1 medium onion, sliced
¼ C. brown sugar
½ C. shredded Colby and Monterey Jack cheese blend

Sprinkle chicken breast halves on both sides with salt and lemon pepper seasoning. Cook chicken in oil in a large nonstick skillet over medium-high heat until chicken is cooked through and the juices run clear, about 12 to 15 minutes. Remove chicken to a plate and keep warm. Cook bacon in same skillet over medium-high heat until crisp. Remove bacon to paper towels to drain, reserving 2 tablespoons bacon drippings in skillet. Add the onion slices and brown sugar to skillet; sauté until onions are golden. Place one cooked chicken breast half on each of four serving plates; top each with two bacon strips and a spoonful of the caramelized onions. Sprinkle 2 tablespoons cheese over each serving.

Tequila Chicken

Makes 6 servings

2 cloves garlic, minced
Grated peel and juice of 1 lime
½ C. tequila
6 boneless, skinless chicken breast halves
1½ C. crushed tortilla chips
1 T. extra-virgin olive oil
⅔ C. Southwestern ranch salad dressing
1 (11 oz.) can whole kernel corn, drained
¾ C. shredded Mexican cheese blend
1 C. salsa, divided
1 medium tomato, chopped, divided
⅔ C. sour cream, divided

Preheat oven to 325°. In a medium bowl, combine garlic, grated peel and juice of lime and tequila; add chicken and chill in refrigerator for 30 minutes to marinate. Cover a baking sheet with aluminum foil. Spread crushed chips over baking sheet in an even layer; bake in oven for 5 minutes or until lightly toasted. Heat oil in a large nonstick skillet over medium-low heat. Add chicken and marinade to skillet; sauté chicken until lightly browned, about 4 minutes on each side. Stir in ranch dressing and simmer for 2 minutes, turning chicken after 1 minute. Sprinkle corn over ingredients in skillet and heat for an additional minute. Sprinkle with cheese and continue to heat until cheese is melted and chicken is cooked through. Place one cooked chicken breast half on each of six serving plates; top each with a generous amount of the toasted chips, salsa, chopped tomato and a dollop of sour cream.

Creamy Basil Chicken

Makes 4 servings

¼ C. milk
¼ C. dry bread crumbs
4 boneless, skinless chicken breast halves
3 T. butter
½ C. chicken broth
1 C. heavy whipping cream
¼ C. chopped roasted red peppers, drained
½ C. grated Parmesan cheese
¼ C. chopped fresh basil
⅛ tsp. pepper

Place milk and bread crumbs in separate shallow bowls. Dip the chicken first into the milk and then into the bread crumbs, turning until evenly coated. Melt butter in a large nonstick skillet over medium-high heat. Add chicken to skillet and fry until chicken is cooked through and evenly browned on all sides. Remove chicken to a plate and keep warm. Add chicken broth to skillet and bring to a boil, stirring to remove any bits stuck to skillet. Stir in heavy cream and roasted peppers; reduce heat and simmer for 1 minute. Stir in Parmesan cheese, basil and pepper; continue to simmer until heated through. Place one cooked chicken breast half on each of four serving plates. Spoon a generous amount of the basil sauce over each serving.

White Wine Chicken with Mushrooms

Makes 4 servings

4 boneless, skinless chicken breast halves
Salt and pepper to taste
2 T. extra-virgin olive oil, divided
1 lb. white mushrooms, sliced thick
4 cloves garlic, halved
½ C. dry white wine
1¾ C. chicken broth
2 T. chopped fresh parsley

Sprinkle chicken on both sides with salt and pepper. Heat 1 tablespoon oil in a large nonstick skillet over high heat. Add chicken to skillet and cook until lightly browned, about 2 to 3 minutes on each side. Remove chicken to a plate and keep warm. Add remaining 1 tablespoon oil to the skillet; stir in mushrooms, garlic and ¼ teaspoon salt. Cover skillet and cook over medium heat for 2 to 3 minutes. Remove lid and increase heat to high. Cook mushrooms, stirring occasionally, until golden, about 4 to 5 minutes. Add wine to skillet and heat for 1 minute, stirring constantly. Reduce heat to medium-high; stir in chicken broth and parsley. Continue to heat until liquid has reduced, about 8 to 10 minutes. Return chicken to skillet, cover and simmer over low heat until chicken is cooked through, about 10 to 12 minutes. Place one cooked chicken breast half on each of four serving plates. Spoon a generous amount of the mushroom sauce over each serving.

Zucchini and Chicken Skillet

Makes 4 servings

4 boneless, skinless chicken breast halves
½ C. flour
½ tsp. Cajun seasoning
½ tsp. salt
Dash of pepper
2 T. extra-virgin olive oil
2 C. sliced zucchini
2 T. lemon juice
½ C. chicken broth
1 large tomato, cut into thin wedges
½ C. chopped roasted red peppers, drained
1 C. prepared Alfredo sauce
Salt and pepper to taste
Hot cooked linguine or fettuccine

Pound chicken breast halves with a mallet to about ¼" thickness. In a small bowl, combine flour, Cajun seasoning, salt and pepper. Dredge chicken in flour mixture. Heat oil in a large nonstick skillet over medium-high heat; add chicken and cook for about 5 minutes on each side. Remove chicken to a plate and keep warm. Add zucchini to skillet and sauté for 2 minutes. Stir lemon juice and chicken broth into skillet. Return chicken to skillet, cover and simmer over medium-low heat for about 15 to 20 minutes or until chicken is cooked through. Add tomato wedges, roasted peppers and Alfredo sauce to skillet, stirring to combine. Continue heating until sauce is hot and bubbly. Place a portion of the cooked pasta on each of four serving plates; top each with one cooked chicken breast half and a generous amount of the sauce.

Chicken in Cilantro Cream Sauce

Makes 4 servings

4 boneless, skinless chicken breast halves
1 tsp. Cajun seasoning, divided
Salt and pepper to taste
2 T. extra-virgin olive oil
½ red bell pepper, sliced
4 to 6 green onions, sliced
1½ C. chicken broth
¼ C. dry white wine
½ C. heavy whipping cream
1 T. butter
½ C. chopped fresh cilantro
½ C. halved cherry tomatoes

Pound chicken breast halves with a mallet to about ¼"
thickness. Sprinkle ½ teaspoon Cajun seasoning, salt and
pepper over both sides of the chicken breast halves. Heat
oil in a large nonstick skillet over medium-high heat; add
chicken and cook for about 5 minutes on each side or until
chicken is cooked through. Remove chicken to a plate and
keep warm. Add bell pepper and green onions to skillet.
Cook, stirring often, until vegetables are tender, about
1 minute. Stir in chicken broth and wine; bring to a boil. Continue
to simmer until juices have reduced to ½ cup. Stir in heavy
cream and butter; heat for 3 minutes. Stir in cilantro, tomatoes
and remaining ½ teaspoon Cajun seasoning. Season to taste
with salt and pepper. Place one cooked chicken breast half on
each of four serving plates. Spoon a generous amount of the
cilantro cream sauce over each serving.

Ham and Chicken Skillet

Makes 4 servings

4 boneless, skinless chicken breast halves
1 tsp. seasoned salt
1 small onion, chopped
3 medium potatoes, cut into ½" cubes
¼ lb. thinly sliced Black Forest ham
3 C. cabbage slaw mix
1 tsp. crushed caraway seed

Sprinkle both sides of chicken breast halves with seasoned salt. Heat a large nonstick skillet over medium-high heat and spray with nonstick cooking spray. Add chicken to skillet, cover andcook for 4 minutes per side or until well browned. Remove chicken to a plate and keep warm. Add onion, potatoes, ham, cabbage and caraway seed to skillet; mix well and top with chicken. Cover skillet and cook for 10 to 15 minutes or until chicken is cooked through.

Easy Cuban Chicken Dinner

Makes 6 servings

¼ C. flour
1½ tsp. salt, divided
Pinch of pepper
6 boneless, skinless chicken breast halves
3 T. butter
1 (14.5 oz.) can stewed tomatoes in liquid
½ C. water
2 T. brown sugar
2 T. white vinegar
2 T. Worcestershire sauce
2 tsp. chili powder
1 tsp. ground mustard
½ tsp. celery seed
1 clove garlic, minced
⅛ tsp. hot pepper sauce

In a shallow bowl, combine flour, ½ teaspoon salt and pepper. Dredge chicken in flour mixture. Melt butter in a large nonstick skillet over medium heat; add chicken and cook for 4 minutes per side or until well browned. Remove chicken to a plate and keep warm. Add tomatoes, water, brown sugar, vinegar, Worcestershire sauce, chili powder, ground mustard, celery seed, garlic, hot pepper sauce and remaining 1 teaspoon salt to skillet. Mix ingredients well and bring to a boil; reduce heat to medium-low and return chicken to skillet. Cover skillet and simmer for 30 to 40 minutes or until chicken is cooked through.

Italian Chicken Florentine

Makes 4 servings

½ C. Italian salad dressing
1 tsp. dried Italian seasoning
4 boneless, skinless chicken breast halves
1 (10 oz.) jar prepared Alfredo sauce
2 C. frozen chopped spinach, thawed and well drained
2 T. extra-virgin olive oil
Hot cooked fettuccine
½ C. grated Parmesan cheese

In a large bowl, combine Italian dressing and Italian seasoning. Add chicken to bowl, turning to cover completely; chill in refrigerator for 30 minutes to marinate. In a separate bowl, combine Alfredo sauce and drained spinach; mix well and set aside. Heat oil in a large nonstick skillet over medium heat. Cook chicken, discarding marinade, in skillet for 5 minutes on each side or until chicken is cooked through. Add Alfredo mixture to skillet and cook until bubbly. Place a portion of the cooked pasta on each of four serving plates; top each with one cooked chicken breast half and a generous amount of the Alfredo and spinach sauce.

Crab-Stuffed Chicken

Makes 4 servings

3 oz. cream cheese, softened
2 T. minced onion
2 T. chopped fresh parsley
1 tsp. chopped fresh dill
1 tsp. minced garlic
⅛ tsp. lemon pepper seasoning
4 oz. fresh crabmeat, flaked
Salt and pepper to taste
1 C. flour
2 eggs, beaten
3 C. fresh bread crumbs
4 boneless, skinless chicken breast halves
2 T. butter
2 T. vegetable oil

In a medium bowl, combine cream cheese, onion, parsley, dill, garlic and lemon pepper seasoning. Add crabmeat and mix until well combined; season with salt and pepper to taste. Cover and chill crab mixture in refrigerator. Place flour, eggs and bread crumbs in three separate shallow dishes. Using a small sharp knife, cut a slit horizontally through the center of each chicken breast half, creating a pocket. Fill each pocket with ¼ of the crab stuffing. Dip each stuffed chicken piece first into the flour, then into the egg and then into the bread crumbs. Heat butter and oil in a large nonstick skillet over medium-high heat. Fry stuffed chicken in skillet for about 10 minutes on each side or until chicken is cooked through and no longer pink. Remove stuffed chicken from skillet and drain on paper towels. Serve immediately.

Fried Lime Chicken

Makes 4 servings

1 egg, beaten
⅔ C. dry bread crumbs
4 boneless, skinless chicken breast halves
2 T. extra-virgin olive oil
Juice of 1 lime
6 T. butter
1 tsp. minced fresh chives
½ tsp. dried dillweed

Place egg and bread crumbs in separate shallow bowls. Dip chicken breast halves first into the egg and then into the bread crumbs, turning to coat both sides. Place coated chicken on a wire rack and let dry for about 10 minutes. Heat oil in a large nonstick skillet over medium heat. Fry chicken in skillet for 3 to 5 minutes on each side or until chicken is cooked through. Remove chicken to a plate and keep warm. Drain grease from skillet. Squeeze lime juice into skillet; cover and cook over low heat until juice boils. Stir butter into skillet until melted; mix in chives and dillweed. Place one fried chicken breast half on each of four serving plates. Spoon a generous amount of the lime sauce over each serving.

Garlic and Mushroom Chicken

4 boneless, skinless chicken breast halves
Salt and pepper to taste
2 T. flour
2 T. extra-virgin olive oil
6 cloves garlic, minced
1 (8 oz.) pkg. sliced fresh mushrooms
¼ C. balsamic vinegar
¾ C. chicken broth
1 bay leaf
¼ tsp. dried thyme
1 T. butter

Season both sides of chicken breast halves with salt and pepper. Place flour in a shallow bowl and season with salt and pepper. Dredge chicken in flour mixture. Heat oil in a large nonstick skillet over medium-high heat; add chicken and sauté until well browned on one side, about 3 minutes. Add garlic and mushrooms to skillet; turn chicken over and cook for another 3 minutes. Stir in vinegar, chicken broth, bay leaf and thyme. Cover skillet and simmer over medium-low heat, stirring occasionally, for 10 minutes or until chicken is cooked through. Remove chicken to a plate and keep warm. Continue simmering the sauce, uncovered, over medium-high heat for about 7 minutes. Stir in the butter and remove the bay leaf. Place one cooked chicken breast half on each of four serving plates. Spoon a generous amount of the mushroom sauce over each serving.

Raspberry Vinaigrette Chicken

Makes 4 servings

2 T. butter
1 T. vegetable oil
4 boneless, skinless chicken breast halves
3 T. green onions, minced
⅓ C. chicken broth
¼ C. raspberry-flavored vinegar
   or raspberry vinaigrette
⅓ C. heavy whipping cream
Salt and pepper to taste

Heat butter and oil in a large saucepan over medium heat; add chicken breast halves and cook for about 6 minutes on each side or until chicken is cooked through and no longer pink. Remove chicken to a plate and keep warm. Add green onions and chicken broth to skillet; simmer for 3 minutes. Stir raspberry vinegar into skillet and bring to a boil; simmer, stirring occasionally, until the mixture thickens. Return chicken to skillet and stir in heavy cream. Heat for 1 minute, turning to coat the chicken pieces with the sauce. Season to taste with salt and pepper. Place one cooked chicken breast half on each of four serving plates. Spoon a generous amount of the cream sauce over each serving.

Apple-Stuffed Chicken Rolls

Makes 4 servings

½ C. chopped apple
2 T. shredded Cheddar cheese
1 T. dry bread crumbs
4 boneless, skinless chicken breast halves
1 T. butter
¼ C. dry white wine
¼ C. plus 1 T. water, divided
1½ tsp. cornstarch
1 T. chopped fresh parsley

In a medium bowl, combine apple, cheese and bread crumbs; mix well and set aside. Pound chicken breast halves with a mallet to about ¼" thickness. Place ¼ of the apple mixture over each chicken piece. Roll up chicken to enclose apple stuffing, securing with toothpicks. Melt butter in a large nonstick skillet over medium heat; add chicken rolls to skillet and cook until browned on all sides. Add wine and ¼ cup water to skillet, stirring gently. Cover skillet and simmer for 15 to 20 minutes or until chicken is cooked through and no longer pink. Place one cooked chicken roll on each of four serving plates and keep warm. In a small bowl, combine remaining 1 tablespoon water and cornstarch. Stir cornstarch mixture into juices in skillet; heat until thickened. Spoon a generous amount of the sauce over each chicken roll. Garnish each serving with a sprinkling of parsley.

Cranberry Orange Chicken

Makes 4 servings

4 boneless, skinless chicken breast halves
½ C. flour
1 tsp. salt
Dash of pepper
1 T. butter
1 T. extra-virgin olive oil
¾ C. orange juice
¼ C. Cointreau or Grand Marnier
½ C. chopped dried cranberries
½ C. sliced green onions

Pound chicken breast halves with a mallet to about ¼" thickness. In a medium bowl, combine flour, salt and pepper. Dredge chicken in flour mixture until evenly coated. Heat butter and oil in a large nonstick skillet over medium-low heat; add chicken to skillet and cook until lightly browned, about 3 minutes on each side. Pour orange juice and Cointreau over chicken in skillet; sprinkle with dried cranberries. Cover skillet and reduce heat to low; simmer for about 20 minutes or until chicken is cooked through. Stir in green onions and heat for an additional minute. Place one cooked chicken breast half on each of four serving plates. Spoon a generous amount of the orange and cranberry sauce over each serving.

Sweet Citrus Chicken

4 boneless, skinless chicken breast halves
½ tsp. five spice powder
½ tsp. salt
¼ tsp. pepper
1 T. sesame oil
¼ C. orange juice
2 T. rice wine vinegar
1 large clove garlic, minced
1 tsp. honey
½ tsp. grated orange zest
2 oranges, peeled, seeded and chopped
2 T. sliced water chestnuts
2 T. minced crystallized ginger
1 small green onion, minced

Sprinkle chicken breast halves on both sides with five spice powder, salt and pepper. Heat oil in a large nonstick skillet over medium-high heat; add chicken to skillet and cook until lightly browned, about 3 minutes on each side. Reduce heat to medium-low. Cover skillet and heat until chicken is cooked through and no longer pink. Remove chicken to a plate and keep warm. Stir orange juice, vinegar, garlic and honey into skillet. Cook, stirring often, until well blended. Mix in orange zest, chopped oranges, water chestnuts, crystallized ginger and green onion; cook until heated through. Place one cooked chicken breast half on each of four serving plates. Spoon a generous amount of the sweet orange sauce over each serving.

Almond Chicken

Makes 6 servings

¼ C. butter
½ C. sliced almonds
¼ C. flour
¼ tsp. dried rosemary
¼ tsp. salt
¼ tsp. pepper
6 boneless, skinless chicken breast halves
½ C. dry white wine

Melt butter in a large nonstick skillet over medium heat; add almonds and cook, stirring often, until lightly browned. Remove almonds with a slotted spoon and set aside. In a small bowl, combine flour, rosemary, salt and pepper. Dredge chicken breast halves in flour mixture. Add chicken to skillet and cook until well browned, about 5 minutes on each side; stir in wine. Cover skillet, reduce heat to medium-low and simmer for 15 minutes or until chicken is cooked through and no longer pink. Remove chicken to a plate and keep warm. Bring juices in skillet to a boil, then stir in almonds. Place one cooked chicken breast half on each of four serving plates. Spoon a generous amount of the almond sauce over each serving.

Maple Pecan Chicken

Makes 4 servings

1 C. chopped pecans
3 T. flour
1 tsp. salt
4 boneless, skinless chicken breast halves
2 T. maple syrup
2 T. butter
1 T. vegetable oil

In a shallow bowl, combine pecans, flour and salt. Brush chicken on all sides with maple syrup. Dredge chicken in pecan mixture until well coated. Heat butter and oil in a large nonstick skillet over medium heat. Add coated chicken and fry for 12 to 15 minutes or until chicken is cooked through and the juices run clear.

Simple Mexican Fried Chicken

Makes 4 servings

4 boneless, skinless chicken breast halves
1 qt. buttermilk
2 (1.25 oz.) pkgs. taco seasoning, divided
1½ C. flour
3 T. extra-virgin olive oil

Place chicken in a large zippered plastic bag; add buttermilk and contents of one taco seasoning packet. Seal bag tightly and shake to mix everything together. Chill in refrigerator overnight to marinate. In a shallow bowl, combine flour and contents of remaining taco seasoning packet. Heat oil in a large nonstick skillet over medium-low heat. Remove chicken from refrigerator and discard marinade. Dredge chicken in flour mixture, turning to coat all sides. Fry chicken in skillet, turning once, until cooked through and the juices run clear, about 15 to 20 minutes.

CHICKEN

Grilled & Broiled

California Grilled Chicken

Makes 4 servings

½ C. coarsely chopped walnuts
1 large fresh nectarine
¼ C. honey
½ C. brown sugar
3 T. lemon juice
½ tsp. ground cinnamon
¼ tsp. ground ginger
4 boneless, skinless chicken breast halves

Heat walnuts in a small skillet over low heat for 3 to 5 minutes, or until lightly toasted. Remove from heat and let cool. Chop walnuts in a food processor until finely ground; set aside. Peel, seed and coarsely chop the nectarine. Process the fruit in a blender or food processor until liquefied. Pour pureed fruit into a large saucepan over low heat; stir in honey, brown sugar, lemon juice, cinnamon and ground ginger. Cook sauce for 8 to 12 minutes or until slightly thickened. Bring mixture to a boil, stirring constantly; remove from heat and let cool. Pour cooled sauce into a large zippered plastic bag. Add walnuts and chicken. Seal bag, removing any air. Shake bag slightly and chill in refrigerator for 1 to 2 hours to marinate. Preheat an outdoor grill to medium-high heat and lightly oil the grate. Grill the chicken, discarding the marinade, for 10 to 12 minutes or until chicken is cooked through, turning once. To broil chicken, place 5" or 6" under preheated oven broiler for 6 minutes on each side or until chicken is cooked through. This recipe also makes a great marinade for pork or shrimp.

Honey Mustard Chicken

Makes 4 servings

1 C. mayonnaise or creamy salad dressing
¼ C. Dijon mustard
¼ C. honey
½ tsp. salt
½ tsp. pepper
4 boneless, skinless chicken breast halves

In a medium bowl, combine mayonnaise, Dijon mustard, honey, salt and pepper. Set aside ½ cup of the sauce in the refrigerator. Pour remaining sauce into a large zippered plastic bag; add chicken. Seal bag, removing any air. Shake bag slightly and chill in refrigerator for at least 2 hours to marinate. Preheat an outdoor grill to medium-high heat and lightly oil the grate. Grill the chicken, discarding the marinade, for 10 to 12 minutes or until chicken is cooked through, turning once. To broil chicken, place 5" or 6" under preheated oven broiler for 6 minutes on each side or until chicken is cooked through. Brush chicken with reserved sauce during last 5 minutes of grilling time or last 2 minutes of broiling time.

Grilled Chicken with Pineapple Salsa

Makes 4 servings

1 (8 oz.) can crushed pineapple, drained
1 (15 oz.) can black beans, drained and rinsed
2 T. lime juice
1 tsp. salt, divided
1 tsp. pepper, divided
½ C. chopped red onion
1 C. chopped tomato
2 cloves garlic, minced
1 tsp. Tabasco sauce
1 T. brown sugar
½ tsp. garlic powder
4 boneless, skinless chicken breast halves

In a medium bowl, combine pineapple, black beans, lime juice, ½ teaspoon salt, ½ teaspoon pepper, onion, tomato and garlic; let sit at room temperature for 15 minutes, then cover and chill in refrigerator. In a small bowl, combine Tabasco sauce, brown sugar, garlic powder, remaining ½ teaspoon salt and ½ teaspoon pepper. Spread mixture over both sides of each chicken breast half. Preheat an outdoor grill to medium-high heat and lightly oil the grate. Grill the chicken for 10 to 12 minutes or until chicken is cooked through, turning once. To broil chicken, place 5" or 6"under preheated oven broiler for 6 minutes on each side or until chicken is cooked through. Serve chicken with the pineapple salsa spooned over top.

Cucumber Relish Chicken

Makes 4 servings

1 cucumber, peeled, seeded and chopped
1 T. chopped fresh parsley
2 T. chopped red onion
½ C. chopped yellow bell pepper
¼ tsp. crushed red pepper flakes
½ tsp. ground cumin
⅛ tsp. chili powder
2 T. extra-virgin olive oil
4 boneless, skinless chicken breast halves

In a medium bowl, combine cucumber, parsley, onion, bell pepper and red pepper flakes; mix well, cover and chill in refrigerator. In a small bowl, combine cumin, chili powder and olive oil. Place chicken in a shallow dish and pour oil mixture over top; cover and chill in refrigerator for at least 1 hour to marinate. Preheat an outdoor grill to medium-high heat and lightly oil the grate. Grill the chicken, discarding the marinade, for 10 to 12 minutes or until chicken is cooked through, turning once. To broil chicken, place 5" or 6" under preheated oven broiler for 6 minutes on each side or until chicken is cooked through. Serve chicken with the cucumber relish spooned over top.

The Best Picnic Chicken

Makes 4 servings

¼ C. ketchup
3 T. apple cider vinegar
2 tsp. brown sugar
1 clove garlic, minced
⅛ tsp. dried thyme
Dash of hot pepper sauce
¼ tsp. pepper
4 boneless, skinless chicken breast halves

In a small saucepan over low heat, combine ketchup, vinegar, brown sugar, garlic, thyme, hot pepper sauce and pepper; bring to a boil over medium heat, stirring often, until sauce thickens, about 5 minutes. Set aside half of the sauce. Brush both sides of chicken lightly with the remaining sauce. Preheat an outdoor grill to medium-high heat and lightly oil the grate. Grill the chicken for 10 to 12 minutes or until chicken is cooked through, turning once. To broil chicken, place 5" or 6" under preheated oven broiler for 6 minutes on each side or until chicken is cooked through. Brush chicken with reserved sauce during last 5 minutes of grilling time or last 2 minutes of broiling time.

Brown Sugar Chicken

Makes 4 servings

2 T. brown sugar
1 T. paprika
2 tsp. onion powder
1½ tsp. salt
1 tsp. chili powder
4 boneless, skinless chicken breast halves

In a small bowl, combine brown sugar, paprika, onion powder, salt and chili powder; rub generously over both sides of each chicken breast half. Preheat an outdoor grill to medium-high heat and lightly oil the grate. Grill the chicken for 10 to 12 minutes or until chicken is cooked through, turning once. To broil chicken, place 5" or 6" under preheated oven broiler for 6 minutes on each side or until chicken is cooked through.

Beer Marinated Chicken

Makes 4 servings

½ C. butter or margarine
1 (12 oz.) can lager beer
1½ tsp. steak seasoning
¾ tsp. seasoning salt
Dash of pepper
4 boneless, skinless chicken breast halves
2 small green bell peppers, thinly sliced

Melt the butter in a large nonstick skillet over medium heat; stir in the beer, steak seasoning, seasoning salt and pepper. Set aside half of the sauce. Brush both sides of chicken generously with the remaining sauce. Preheat an outdoor grill to medium-low heat and lightly oil the grate. Grill the chicken for 20 minutes or until the chicken is cooked through, turning once. To broil chicken, place 5" or 6" under preheated oven broiler for 6 minutes on each side or until chicken is cooked through. Brush chicken with reserved sauce during last 10 minutes of grilling time or last 2 minutes of broiling time. To serve, top each chicken breast half with bell pepper slices.

Jalapeño Chicken Rolls

Makes 6 servings

6 boneless, skinless chicken breast halves
1 (16 oz.) bottle Italian salad dressing
3 fresh jalapeño peppers, halved
   lengthwise and seeded
3 oz. cream cheese, softened
6 slices bacon

Pound chicken breast halves with a mallet to about ¼"
thickness. Place chicken in a shallow dish; pour Italian dressing
over top. Cover dish and chill in refrigerator for at least 2 hours
to marinate. Stuff each jalapeño half with some of the cream
cheese. Roll one chicken breast half around each stuffed pepper,
discarding the marinade. Wrap one slice of bacon around each
chicken roll, securing with toothpicks. Preheat an outdoor grill
to medium-low heat and lightly oil the grate. Grill the chicken for
20 minutes or until chicken is cooked through and the bacon is
browned. To broil chicken, place 5" or 6" under preheated oven
broiler for 6 minutes on each side or until chicken is cooked
through and bacon is browned.

Deliciously Simple Soy Chicken

Makes 4 servings

1 C. soy sauce
1 C. beer
1 C. water
1 clove garlic, minced
Salt and pepper to taste
4 boneless, skinless chicken breast halves

In a large bowl, combine soy sauce, beer, water and garlic; season to taste with salt and pepper. Add chicken to bowl; cover and chill in refrigerator for up to 8 hours to marinate, turning once. Preheat an outdoor grill to medium-high heat and lightly oil the grate. Grill the chicken, discarding the marinade, for 10 to 12 minutes or until chicken is cooked through, turning once. To broil chicken, place 5" or 6" under preheated oven broiler for 6 minutes on each side or until chicken is cooked through.

Rosemary Lemon Chicken

Makes 4 servings

½ C. lemon juice
2 T. extra-virgin olive oil
2 T. dried rosemary
4 boneless, skinless chicken breast halves
1 lemon, sliced

Combine lemon juice, oil and rosemary in a large zippered plastic bag; add chicken and lemon slices. Seal bag, removing any air. Shake bag slightly and chill in refrigerator for up to 8 hours to marinate. Preheat an outdoor grill to medium-high heat and lightly oil the grate. Remove the chicken from the refrigerator and discard the marinade. It is desirable for some of the rosemary to stick to the chicken. Grill the chicken for 10 to 12 minutes or until chicken is cooked through, turning once. To broil chicken, place 5" or 6" under preheated oven broiler for 6 minutes on each side or until chicken is cooked through.

Asian Ginger Chicken

Makes 4 servings

¼ C. soy sauce
4 tsp. dark sesame oil
2 T. honey
3 slices fresh gingerroot
2 cloves garlic, crushed
4 boneless, skinless chicken breast halves

In a small microwave-safe bowl, combine soy sauce, oil, honey, gingerroot and garlic. Heat for 1 minute, then stir. Heat for another 30 seconds, being careful not to let mixture boil. Place chicken in a shallow dish; pour sauce mixture over top. Cover dish and chill in refrigerator for at least 30 minutes to marinate. Preheat an outdoor grill to medium-high heat and lightly oil the grate. Remove chicken from refrigerator and pour marinade into a small saucepan over medium-high heat; bring to a boil for 5 minutes. Grill the chicken for 10 to 12 minutes or until chicken is cooked through, turning once. To broil chicken, place 5" or 6" under preheated oven broiler for 6 minutes on each side or until chicken is cooked through. Brush chicken with boiled sauce during last 5 minutes of grilling time or last 2 minutes of broiling time.

Caribbean Grilled Chicken

Makes 6 servings

¼ C. orange juice
1 tsp. grated orange zest
1 T. extra-virgin olive oil
1 T. lime juice
1 tsp. minced fresh gingerroot
2 cloves garlic, minced
¼ tsp. hot pepper sauce
½ tsp. chopped fresh oregano
6 boneless, skinless chicken breast halves

In a blender, combine orange juice, orange zest, oil, lime juice, gingerroot, garlic, hot pepper sauce and oregano; process until well blended. Place chicken in a shallow dish; pour sauce mixture over top. Cover dish and chill in refrigerator for at least 2 hours to marinate. Preheat an outdoor grill to medium-high heat and lightly oil the grate. Grill the chicken, discarding the marinade, for 10 to 12 minutes or until chicken is cooked through, turning once. To broil chicken, place 5" or 6" under preheated oven broiler for 6 minutes on each side or until chicken is cooked through.

Chicken with Raspberry Sauce

Makes 4 servings

4 boneless, skinless chicken breast halves
2 T. balsamic vinegar
1½ tsp. salt, divided
½ tsp. plus ⅛ tsp. pepper, divided
2 C. fresh raspberries, divided
¼ C. raspberry jam
2 T. sherry or wine vinegar
½ tsp. dried tarragon

Pound chicken breast halves with a mallet to about ¼" thickness. Place chicken in a shallow dish; sprinkle balsamic vinegar, 1 teaspoon salt and ½ teaspoon pepper over top. Cover dish and chill in refrigerator for at least 30 minutes to marinate. Set aside a few raspberries for garnish. In a large saucepan over medium heat, combine remaining raspberries, jam, vinegar, tarragon, remaining ½ teaspoon salt and remaining ⅛ teaspoon pepper; bring to a boil. Reduce heat to low and let sauce simmer for about 5 minutes, stirring often. Remove from heat and let cool slightly. Strain sauce into a bowl through a fine-holed sieve; set aside and keep warm. Preheat an outdoor grill to medium-high heat and lightly oil the grate. Grill the chicken, discarding the marinade, for 10 to 12 minutes or until chicken is cooked through, turning once. To broil chicken, place 5" or 6" under preheated oven broiler for 6 minutes on each side or until chicken is cooked through. Serve chicken with the raspberry sauce spooned over top. Garnish with reserved berries.

Bourbon Chicken

Makes 4 servings

1 tsp. dried parsley flakes
1 tsp. dried thyme
3 T. bourbon
½ C. maple syrup
1 T. vegetable oil
4 boneless, skinless chicken breast halves

In a medium bowl, combine parsley flakes, thyme, bourbon, maple syrup and oil. Place chicken in a shallow dish; pour bourbon mixture over top. Cover dish and chill in refrigerator for at least 2 hours to marinate. Preheat an outdoor grill to medium-high heat and lightly oil the grate. Remove chicken from refrigerator and pour marinade into a small saucepan over medium-high heat; bring to a boil for 5 minutes. Grill the chicken for 10 to 12 minutes or until the chicken is cooked through, turning once. To broil chicken, place 5" or 6" under preheated oven broiler for 6 minutes on each side or until chicken is cooked through. Brush chicken with boiled sauce during last 5 minutes of grilling time or last 2 minutes of broiling time.

Easy Garlic Ranch Chicken

Makes 4 servings

1 C. ranch dressing
2 T. minced garlic
1 T. chopped fresh basil
4 skinless, boneless chicken breast halves

In a large zippered plastic bag, combine ranch dressing, garlic and basil; add chicken. Seal bag, removing any air. Shake bag slightly and chill in refrigerator for 30 minutes to marinate. Preheat an outdoor grill to medium-high heat and lightly oil the grate. Grill the chicken, discarding the marinade, for 10 to 12 minutes or until chicken is cooked through, turning once. To broil chicken, place 5" or 6" under preheated oven broiler for 6 minutes on each side or until chicken is cooked through.

Minty Melon Grilled Chicken

Makes 4 servings

½ tsp. ground allspice
¼ tsp. ground nutmeg
½ tsp. salt
¼ tsp. pepper
4 boneless, skinless chicken breast halves
¼ C. mint jelly, melted
1 T. lime juice
1 C. diced cantaloupe
1 C. diced honeydew melon
2 T. minced red onion
2 T. chopped fresh mint
2 T. minced crystallized ginger
1 stalk celery, diced
½ tsp. grated lime zest

In a small bowl, combine allspice, nutmeg, salt and pepper; rub over both sides of each chicken breast half. In a separate bowl, combine melted jelly and lime juice. Transfer 1 tablespoon of the jelly mixture to a medium bowl; add cantaloupe, honeydew, onion, mint, ginger, celery and lime zest. Mix melon relish, cover and chill in refrigerator. Preheat an outdoor grill to medium-high heat and lightly oil the grate. Grill the chicken for 10 to 12 minutes or until chicken is cooked through, turning once. To broil chicken, place 5" or 6" under preheated oven broiler for 6 minutes on each side or until chicken is cooked through. Brush chicken with remaining jelly glaze during last 5 minutes of grilling time or last 2 minutes of broiling time. Serve chicken with the melon relish spooned over top.

Can't Beat It BBQ Chicken

Makes 6 servings

½ C. Worcestershire sauce
1 tsp. Cajun seasoning
1 tsp. garlic powder
2½ T. brown sugar
1½ T. ketchup
6 boneless, skinless chicken breast halves

In a large bowl, combine Worcestershire sauce, Cajun seasoning, garlic powder, brown sugar and ketchup; mix well. Add chicken to bowl and turn until well coated; cover and chill in refrigerator for up to 8 hours to marinate. Preheat an outdoor grill to medium-high heat and lightly oil the grate. Grill the chicken, discarding the marinade, for 10 to 12 minutes or until chicken is cooked through, turning once. To broil chicken, place 5" or 6" under preheated oven broiler for 6 minutes on each side or until chicken is cooked through.

Creamy Italian Grilled Chicken

Makes 4 servings

1½ C. mayonnaise or creamy salad dressing
1 C. Italain salad dressing
¼ tsp. cayenne pepper
4 boneless, skinless chicken breast halves

In a medium bowl, combine mayonnaise, Italian dressing and cayenne pepper. Add chicken to bowl and turn until well coated; cover and chill in refrigerator for up to 2 hours to marinate. Preheat an outdoor grill to medium-high heat and lightly oil the grate. Grill the chicken, discarding the marinade, for 10 to 12 minutes or until chicken is cooked through, turning once. To broil chicken, place 5" or 6" under preheated oven broiler for 6 minutes on each side or until chicken is cooked through.

Margaritaville Chicken

Makes 4 servings

4 boneless, skinless chicken breast halves
1 C. bottled margarita mix

In a large zippered plastic bag, combine chicken and margarita mix. Seal bag, removing any air. Shake bag slightly and chill in refrigerator for up to 8 hours to marinate. Preheat an outdoor grill to medium-high heat and lightly oil the grate. Grill the chicken, discarding the marinade, for 10 to 12 minutes or until chicken is cooked through, turning once. To broil chicken, place 5" or 6" under preheated oven broiler for 6 minutes on each side or until chicken is cooked through.

Tangy Grilled Chicken

Makes 4 servings

1 C. Worcestershire sauce
1 C. vegetable oil
1 C. lemon juice
1 tsp. garlic powder
4 boneless, skinless chicken breast halves

In a medium bowl, whisk together Worcestershire sauce, oil, lemon juice and garlic powder. Place chicken in a shallow dish; pour Worcestershire mixture over top. Cover dish and chill in refrigerator for at least 6 hours to marinate. Preheat an outdoor grill to medium-high heat and lightly oil the grate. Grill the chicken, discarding the marinade, for 10 to 12 minutes or until chicken is cooked through, turning once. To broil chicken, place 5" or 6"under preheated oven broiler for 6 minutes on each side or until chicken is cooked through.

Herbed Garlic Chicken Packs

Makes 4 servings

6 cloves garlic, crushed
2 tsp. dried tarragon
½ tsp. salt
1 T. pepper
½ C. extra-virgin olive oil
4 boneless, skinless chicken breast halves

In a small bowl, whisk together garlic, tarragon, salt, pepper and oil. Set aside half of the mixture in the refrigerator. Place each chicken breast half on a 10" sheet of aluminum foil. Brush the remaining oil mixture generously over each chicken piece. Wrap the foil around the chicken tightly to seal. Preheat an outdoor grill to medium-high heat. Place the foil packets on the grill, cover and cook for about 30 to 40 minutes. Carefully remove the packets from the grill and open slowly, being careful to avoid any escaping hot steam. Place unwrapped chicken directly on grill and brush with reserved oil mixture. Grill for 5 minutes, turning once.

Veggie Chicken Packs

Makes 4 servings

½ C. vegetable oil
¼ C. apple cider vinegar
1 T. garlic powder
1 tsp. pepper
½ tsp. salt
½ tsp. dried basil
½ tsp. dried thyme
4 boneless, skinless chicken breast halves
4 large potatoes, peeled and cut into ¼" slices
2 large onions, cut into ¼" slices
2 large green bell peppers, cut into ¼" strips
2 C. sliced button mushrooms

In a small bowl, combine oil, vinegar, garlic powder, pepper, salt, basil and thyme; set aside. Place each chicken breast half on a 12" sheet of aluminum foil. Top each chicken piece with an even amount of the potatoes, onions, bell peppers and mushrooms. Ladle ¼ of the oil mixture over ingredients in each packet. Fold foil up and over packets, sealing at the edges and top. It is desirable to have some room inside the packets for the air to circulate. Place the foil packets on the grill, cover and cook for about 30 to 40 minutes or until chicken is cooked through. Carefully remove the packets from the grill and open slowly, being careful to avoid any escaping hot steam. Transfer the contents of each packet to a serving plate.

Spicy Chicken Sandwiches

Makes 4 servings

4 boneless, skinless chicken breast halves
¼ tsp. salt
¼ tsp. pepper
4 slices Havarti or Monterey Jack cheese
½ C. peach preserves
¼ tsp. crushed red pepper flakes
4 French dinner rolls, split

Pound chicken breast halves with a mallet to about ¼" thickness; sprinkle with salt and pepper. Preheat an outdoor grill to medium-high heat and lightly oil the grate. Grill the chicken for 10 to 12 minutes or until chicken is cooked through, turning once. To broil chicken, place 5" or 6" under preheated oven broiler for 6 minutes on each side or until chicken is cooked through. Place one slice of cheese over each chicken breast and grill or broil for 1 more minute or until the cheese is slightly melted. In a small bowl, combine peach preserves and red pepper flakes. Place one chicken breast half on the bottom half of each roll; top with about 2 tablespoons of the preserves mixture. Cover with top halves of rolls to make sandwiches.

Chicken and Sun-Dried Tomato Subs

Makes 6 servings

6 boneless, skinless chicken breast halves
2 T. extra-virgin olive oil
Salt and pepper to taste
¼ tsp. garlic powder
¼ tsp. onion powder
¼ tsp. dried oregano
¼ tsp. crushed red pepper flakes
6 hoagie rolls, split
1 (8 oz.) jar chopped sun-dried tomatoes in oil, oil reserved
1 (4 oz.) can sliced black olives, drained

Pound chicken breast halves with a mallet to about ¼" thickness. Brush chicken pieces lightly with oil and sprinkle each with salt, pepper, garlic powder, onion powder, oregano and red pepper flakes. Preheat an outdoor grill to medium-high heat and lightly oil the grate. Grill the chicken for 10 to 12 minutes or until chicken is cooked through, turning once. To broil chicken, place 5" or 6" under preheated oven broiler for 6 minutes on each side or until chicken is cooked through. Place one chicken breast half on the bottom half of each roll. In a medium bowl, combine drained tomatoes, olives and 2½ tablespoons oil from tomatoes. Spoon a generous amount of the tomato mixture over the chicken on each roll; cover with top halves of rolls to make sandwiches.

Reuben Grilled Chicken

2 T. ground mustard
⅛ tsp. pepper
4 boneless, skinless chicken breast halves
4 slices Swiss cheese
4 slices rye bread, toasted
2 C. prepared cole slaw

In a small bowl, combine ground mustard and pepper; rub over both sides of each chicken breast half. Preheat an outdoor grill to medium-high heat and lightly oil the grate. Grill the chicken for 10 to 12 minutes or until chicken is cooked through, turning once. To broil chicken, place 5" or 6" under preheated oven broiler for 6 minutes on each side or until chicken is cooked through. Place one slice of cheese over each chicken breast and grill or broil for 1 more minute or until the cheese is slightly melted. Place one chicken breast half on each slice of toasted rye bread; top each with about ½ cup prepared cole slaw. Serve as open-faced sandwiches.

CHICKEN

Baked

Basic Breaded Chicken

Makes 4 servings

1 C. sour cream
¼ C. lemon juice
½ tsp. Worcestershire sauce
1½ tsp. celery salt
1 tsp. paprika
Garlic powder to taste
1½ tsp. salt
¼ tsp. pepper
4 boneless, skinless chicken breast halves
¾ to 1 C. dry bread crumbs
¼ C. butter, melted

In a large bowl, combine sour cream, lemon juice, Worcestershire sauce, celery salt, paprika, garlic powder, salt and pepper. Add chicken pieces to bowl, turning until completely coated. Cover bowl and refrigerate chicken for 8 hours or overnight. Preheat oven to 350°. Arrange chicken in a single layer in a lightly greased 9 x 13" baking dish, discarding marinade. Sprinkle bread crumbs over chicken and spoon melted butter over top. Bake, uncovered, for 1 hour or until chicken is cooked through and the juices run clear.

Easy Swiss Chicken

Makes 4 servings

4 boneless, skinless chicken breast halves
Pepper to taste
4 slices Swiss cheese
1 (10.7 oz.) can cream of chicken soup
¼ C. milk
1 C. dry bread crumbs
3 T. butter, melted

Preheat oven to 350°. Place chicken in a single layer in a lightly greased 9 x 13" baking dish; season with pepper to taste. Top each chicken breast half with one slice of cheese. In a medium bowl, combine soup and milk; pour over chicken. Sprinkle bread crumbs over chicken and spoon melted butter over top. Bake, covered, for 30 minutes. Uncover chicken and bake for an additional 20 minutes or until chicken is cooked through and the juices run clear.

Baked Chicken in White Sauce

Makes 4 servings

4 boneless, skinless chicken breast halves
2 (10.7 oz.) cans cream of celery soup
1 C. sour cream
⅓ C. white wine

Preheat oven to 350°. Place chicken in a single layer in a lightly greased 9 x 13" baking dish. In a medium bowl, combine soup, sour cream and wine; mix well and pour over chicken. Cover pan with aluminum foil. Bake, covered, for 1 hour or until chicken is cooked through and the juices run clear.

Crunchy Italian Chicken

Makes 6 servings

2 C. sour cream
2 C. crushed cornflakes cereal
1 tsp. Italian seasoning
6 boneless, skinless chicken breast halves
6 T. butter, melted

Preheat oven to 350°. Place sour cream in a shallow bowl. In a separate shallow bowl, combine crushed cereal and Italian seasoning. Coat chicken generously in sour cream then dip in crushed cereal, turning to coat both sides. Place chicken in a single layer in a lightly greased 9 x 13" baking dish. Drizzle melted butter over chicken. Bake, uncovered, for 1 hour or until chicken is cooked through and the juices run clear.

Curried Dijon Chicken

Makes 4 servings

⅓ C. butter, melted
⅓ C. honey
¼ C. Dijon mustard
4 tsp. curry powder
Pinch of cayenne pepper
4 boneless, skinless chicken breast halves

In a medium bowl, combine butter, honey, Dijon mustard, curry powder and cayenne pepper; mix well. Place chicken in a single layer in a lightly greased 9 x 13" baking dish; pour butter mixture over top. Cover dish and refrigerate chicken for 4 hours or overnight. Preheat oven to 375°. Bake, covered, for 20 minutes. Uncover chicken and bake for an additional 10 to 20 minutes or until chicken is cooked through and the juices run clear.

Brown Sugar Bourbon Chicken

Makes 4 servings

4 boneless, skinless chicken breast halves
1 tsp. ground ginger
½ C. soy sauce
2 T. dried minced onion
½ C. brown sugar
¼ to ⅓ C. bourbon
½ tsp. garlic powder

Place chicken in a single layer in a lightly greased 9 x 13" baking dish. In a small bowl, combine ginger, soy sauce, dried onion, brown sugar, bourbon and garlic powder; pour over chicken. Cover dish and refrigerate chicken for 8 hours or overnight. Preheat oven to 325°. Bake, uncovered, for 1½ hours, basting frequently with the pan juices, until chicken is cooked through and the juices run clear.

Peppered Chicken in Creamy Mustard Sauce

Makes 4 servings

4 boneless, skinless chicken breast halves
2 tsp. extra-virgin olive oil
¼ tsp. salt
2 tsp. pepper
2 tsp. cornstarch
⅓ C. sour cream
1 C. chicken broth
¼ C. white grape juice
¼ C. chopped green onions
2 tsp. Dijon mustard

Preheat oven to 425°. Rub both sides of each chicken breast half with oil; place in a single layer in a lightly greased 9 x 13" baking dish. Sprinkle chicken with salt and pepper. Bake, uncovered, for 15 to 20 minutes or until chicken is cooked through and the juices run clear. Meanwhile, in a small bowl, combine cornstarch and sour cream until smooth; set aside. In a small saucepan over medium heat, combine chicken broth, grape juice and green onions; bring to a boil for 4 to 5 minutes or until liquid is reduced to 1 cup. Gradually whisk sour cream mixture into the saucepan; return to a boil, stirring constantly, for 2 minutes or until thickened. Remove saucepan from heat and stir in Dijon mustard. Place one cooked chicken breast half on each of four serving plates. Spoon a generous amount of the sauce over each serving.

Parmesan Baked Chicken

Makes 4 servings

¼ C. Dijon mustard
2 T. apple juice
1 clove garlic, minced
1 C. fresh bread crumbs
½ C. grated Parmesan cheese
1 tsp. dried parsley flakes
1½ tsp. butter, melted
⅛ tsp. salt
Pinch of pepper
4 boneless, skinless chicken breast halves

Preheat oven to 375°. Line a 9 x 13" baking dish with aluminum foil; set aside. In a shallow bowl, combine Dijon mustard, apple juice and garlic. In a separate bowl, combine bread crumbs, Parmesan cheese, dried parsley, melted butter, salt and pepper. Coat chicken generously in mustard mixture, then dip in crumb mixture, turning to coat both sides. Place chicken in prepared dish. Bake, uncovered, for 25 to 35 minutes or until chicken is cooked through and the juices run clear.

Cayenne Chicken with Avocado Salsa

Makes 4 servings

1 tsp. salt
¼ tsp. pepper
¼ tsp. cayenne pepper
4 boneless, skinless chicken breast halves
1 medium red onion, finely diced
2 T. lime juice
1 avocado, peeled, pitted and chopped

Preheat oven to 400°. In a small bowl, combine salt, pepper and cayenne pepper; rub over both sides of each chicken breast half. Place chicken in a single layer in a lightly greased 9 x 13" baking dish. Bake, uncovered, for 25 to 35 minutes or until chicken is cooked through and the juices run clear. Meanwhile, in a medium bowl, combine onion, lime juice and avocado; season with salt and pepper to taste. Place one cooked chicken breast half on each of four serving plates; top each with a generous amount of the avocado salsa.

Chipotle Chicken

Makes 4 servings

2 C. fresh or frozen whole kernel corn
3 C. frozen diced hash brown potatoes
1 (14.5 oz.) can diced tomatoes with basil,
    garlic and oregano
2 chipotle peppers in adobo sauce, chopped
¾ tsp. chili powder, divided
¾ tsp. ground cumin, divided
½ tsp. dried oregano
1 T. extra-virgin olive oil
4 boneless, skinless chicken breast halves
¼ tsp. salt
¾ C. shredded Colby and Monterey Jack cheese

Preheat oven to 375°. Coat a large nonstick skillet with nonstick cooking spray and place over medium-high heat. Add corn and sauté for 5 minutes or until corn starts to brown. Stir in hash browns and cook, stirring often, for 5 to 8 minutes or until potatoes begin to brown. Stir in tomatoes with liquid, chipotle peppers, ½ teaspoon chili powder, ½ teaspoon cumin and oregano; sauté until heated through. Spread mixture in an even layer in a lightly greased 9 x 13" baking dish. Wipe skillet clean. Heat oil in same skillet over medium-high heat. Sprinkle chicken evenly with salt, remaining ¼ teaspoon chili powder and remaining ¼ teaspoon cumin. Sauté chicken in skillet until browned, about 3 minutes on each side. Place chicken over ingredients in baking dish. Bake, uncovered, for 25 to 35 minutes or until chicken is cooked through and the juices run clear. Sprinkle cheese immediately over chicken. To serve, place a generous amount of the corn and hash brown mixture on each of four serving plates; top each with one cooked chicken breast half.

Chicken with Caramelized Onions

Makes 4 servings

4 boneless, skinless chicken breast halves
1 T. extra-virgin olive oil
2 medium onions, sliced
6 cloves garlic, minced
⅓ C. brown sugar
2 T. white wine vinegar

Preheat oven to 450°. Place chicken breast halves in a single layer in a lightly greased 9 x 13″ baking dish; set aside. Heat oil in a nonstick skillet over medium-low heat. Add onions and garlic; sauté for 6 to 8 minutes or until softened. Stir in brown sugar and vinegar until dissolved. Continue to heat, stirring constantly, until liquid evaporates, about 7 to 9 minutes. Remove from heat and spread over chicken in baking dish; cover loosely with foil. Bake, covered, for 20 to 25 minutes or until chicken is cooked through and the juices run clear.

Broccoli, Chicken and Rice Casserole

Makes 4 servings

1 (6 oz.) box rice broccoli au gratin
2 C. boiling water
4 boneless, skinless chicken breast halves
¼ tsp. garlic powder
2 C. frozen broccoli florets, thawed
1 C. shredded Cheddar cheese

Preheat oven to 425°. In a 9 x 13" baking dish, combine rice and seasoning packet; stir in boiling water and mix well. Place chicken breast halves over rice; sprinkle with garlic powder. Bake, covered, for 30 minutes. Stir in broccoli, cover and return to oven for 4 to 8 minutes or until the chicken is cooked through and the broccoli is heated. Sprinkle cheese over chicken and broccoli. Bake, uncovered, for 5 minutes or until the cheese is melted.

Fiesta Chicken

Makes 4 servings

4 boneless, skinless chicken breast halves
1 (15 oz.) can black beans, drained and rinsed
1 (16 oz.) jar salsa
2 C. whole kernel corn
Coarsely broken blue or yellow corn chips
Shredded lettuce, sour cream and
  shredded cheese for garnish

Preheat oven to 400°. Place chicken breast halves in a single layer in a lightly greased 9 x 13" baking dish. Prick chicken with a fork. Pour beans, salsa and corn over chicken. Bake, uncovered, for 25 to 35 minutes or until chicken is cooked through and the juices run clear. Place one cooked chicken breast half on each of four serving plates. Surround each with shredded lettuce and broken chips. Top each with a dollop of sour cream and sprinkling of cheese.

Balsamic Chicken with Pears

Makes 4 servings

2 pears, cored and thinly sliced
½ C. thinly sliced red onion
1 T. extra-virgin olive oil
½ tsp. dried thyme
½ tsp. salt
¼ tsp. pepper
4 boneless, skinless chicken breast halves
1 T. balsamic vinegar

Preheat oven to 450°. Place pear and onion slices in a single layer in a lightly greased 9 x 13" baking dish. In a small bowl, combine oil, thyme, salt and pepper; spoon half over the pears and onions. Cover dish tightly with foil and bake for 10 minutes. Meanwhile, coat chicken breast halves with remaining oil mixture. Uncover dish and place chicken over pears and onions. Drizzle vinegar over chicken. Bake, uncovered, for 20 to 25 minutes or until chicken is cooked through and the juices run clear.

Spinach Chicken Bake

Makes 4 servings

1 (6 oz.) bag baby spinach, rinsed
Salt and pepper to taste
¼ C. chicken broth
4 boneless, skinless chicken breast halves
Creole or Cajun seasoning to taste
1 large tomato, diced
4 green onions, sliced

Preheat oven to 350°. Place spinach in a single layer in a lightly greased 9 x 13" baking dish; sprinkle with salt and pepper. Pour chicken broth over spinach. Pound chicken breast halves with a mallet to about ¾" thickness. Season chicken to taste with Creole seasoning, salt and pepper; place over spinach. Sprinkle tomato and green onions over chicken. Bake, covered, for 25 minutes. Uncover chicken and bake for an additional 15 to 25 minutes or until chicken is cooked through and the juices run clear.

Walnut Chicken

Makes 6 servings

6 boneless, skinless chicken breast halves
Salt and pepper to taste
Garlic powder to taste
2 eggs, beaten well
1 C. ground walnuts
¾ C. crushed seasoned croutons

Preheat oven to 400°. Pound chicken breast halves with a mallet to about ¾" thickness; sprinkle with salt, pepper and garlic powder. Place eggs in a shallow dish. Combine ground walnuts and croutons in a separate shallow dish. Dip chicken breast halves first into the eggs, letting any excess drip off, and then into the walnut mixture, turning until well coated on both sides. Place coated chicken in a single layer in a lightly greased 9 x 13" baking dish. Bake, uncovered, for 25 to 35 minutes or until chicken is cooked through and the juices run clear.

Florentine Chicken Casserole

Makes 6 servings

6 boneless, skinless chicken breast halves
8 oz. medium pasta shells, cooked and drained
2 T. extra-virgin olive oil
2 tsp. dried basil, divided
1 (16 oz.) tub small curd cottage cheese
1 (10 oz.) box frozen chopped spinach,
   thawed and drained
2 (8 oz.) bag shredded Italian cheese blend, divided
1 (1.6 oz.) env. Alfredo sauce mix, prepared, divided

Preheat oven to 350°. Pound chicken breast halves with a mallet to about ¼" to ½" thickness. In a medium bowl, toss cooked pasta with oil and 1 teaspoon basil. Spread pasta in an even layer in a lightly greased 9 x 13" baking dish. Place three chicken breast halves over the pasta. Spread cottage cheese over chicken and spread spinach over cottage cheese. Sprinkle half of the cheese over the spinach and spread half of the prepared Alfredo sauce over the cheese. Sprinkle with remaining 1 teaspoon basil. Place remaining three chicken breast halves on top. Spread remaining Alfredo sauce over chicken and top with remaining cheese. Bake, uncovered, for 45 minutes or until chicken is cooked through and ingredients are hot.

Beefed Up Chicken Casserole

Makes 4 to 6 servings

1 (2.5 oz.) jar dried beef
4 to 6 boneless, skinless chicken breast halves
4 to 6 strips bacon
1 (10.7 oz.) can cream of chicken soup
1 (16 oz.) tub sour cream
1 (8 oz.) pkg. cream cheese, softened
Pepper to taste

Preheat oven to 375°. Place dried beef in a single layer over the bottom of a lightly greased 9 x 13" baking dish. Wrap each chicken breast half with one bacon slice; lay over dried beef. In a medium bowl, combine soup, sour cream, cream cheese and pepper; pour over chicken. Bake, uncovered, for 25 to 35 minutes or until chicken is cooked through and the juices run clear.

Artichoke Chicken Wellington

Makes 4 servings

1 (8 oz.) pkg. cream cheese, softened
½ lb. Kalamata olives, pitted
1 clove garlic, minced
2 tsp. capers
1 (14 oz.) can artichoke hearts, drained
4 boneless, skinless chicken breast halves
Salt and pepper to taste
1 T. extra-virgin olive oil
2 sheets frozen puff pastry, thawed

Preheat oven to 400°. In a food processor, combine cream cheese, olives, garlic, capers and artichoke hearts; pulse until finely chopped and set aside. Season both sides of each chicken breast half with salt and pepper. Heat oil in a large nonstick skillet over medium-high heat. Sear chicken until golden brown, about 3 or 4 minutes per side; remove chicken to a plate and keep warm. Unroll puff pastry sheets and smooth any creases. Cut each square in half to make four pieces. Place one chicken breast half over each puff pastry piece; spread each with ¼ of the artichoke mixture. Fold pastry over and seal the edges to enclose chicken. Bake for 20 to 30 minutes or until pastry is puffed and chicken is cooked through.

Red Pepper Chicken with White Cheese Sauce

Makes 4 to 6 servings

4 to 6 boneless, skinless chicken breast halves
1 medium sweet onion, diced
1 clove garlic, minced
¼ C. diced red bell pepper or roasted red pepper
1 T. extra-virgin olive oil
2 T. butter
2 T. flour
1½ C. milk
½ tsp. salt
Dash of pepper
1 C. shredded or diced Havarti,
   Gouda or Jack cheese

Preheat oven to 350°. Place chicken breast halves in a single layer in a lightly greased 9 x 13" baking dish. In a medium bowl, toss together onion, garlic, bell pepper and oil; spread over chicken. Bake, uncovered, for 20 minutes. Meanwhile, melt butter in a medium saucepan over medium-low heat. Stir in flour until smooth. Mix in milk, salt and pepper. Cook, stirring constantly, until sauce is thickened. Stir in cheese until melted. Spoon cheese sauce over chicken. Return to oven and bake, uncovered, until chicken is cooked through and the juices run clear, about 20 to 25 minutes.

Moroccan Chicken

Makes 4 servings

1 (15 oz.) can garbanzo beans, drained and rinsed
1 C. chicken broth
¾ C. halved dried apricots
1 cinnamon stick
4 boneless, skinless chicken breast halves
½ tsp. salt
¼ tsp. pepper
2 T. chopped fresh parsley

Preheat oven to 425°. In a lightly greased 9 x 13" baking dish, combine garbanzo beans, chicken broth, apricots and cinnamon stick. Arrange chicken breast halves in an even layer over ingredients in pan. Sprinkle salt and pepper over top. Spray top of chicken lightly with nonstick cooking spray. Bake, covered, for 25 minutes or until chicken is cooked through and the juices run clear. Before serving, remove cinnamon stick and sprinkle chicken with parsley.

Prosciutto Chicken in Cran-Orange Jus

Makes 4 servings

¼ C. butter, softened
2 cloves garlic, minced
4 boneless, skinless chicken breast halves
8 thin slices prosciutto
1 ¼ C. chicken broth
½ C. orange juice
½ C. sugar
1 ½ C. fresh cranberries

Preheat oven to 350°. In a small bowl, combine butter and garlic. Cut a slit in the side of each chicken breast half to make a pocket; fill with garlic butter. Wrap each chicken breast half with two slices of prosciutto. Place wrapped chicken in a single layer in a lightly greased 9 x 13" baking dish, seam side down. Pour chicken broth over chicken. Bake, uncovered, for 30 to 40 minutes or until chicken is cooked through and the juices run clear. Remove chicken to a plate and keep warm by covering with aluminum foil. In a medium saucepan over medium heat, combine cooking liquid from baking dish, orange juice and sugar; bring to a simmer. Stir in cranberries and heat until berries begin to pop, about 10 minutes. Strain juice into a bowl to remove any solids, pressing down on the cranberries to release the juice. To serve, cut each chicken breast half into a few slices and place on serving plates. Drizzle the cran-orange sauce over the chicken and serve immediately.

Chicken and Mushrooms in Almond Sauce

Makes 4 servings

4 boneless, skinless chicken breast halves
Salt and pepper to taste
1 egg
½ C. water
2 C. finely chopped almonds
¼ C. butter
3 T. extra-virgin olive oil

1 lb. fresh mushrooms
1 onion, sliced into rings
2 cloves garlic, crushed
1 C. heavy whipping cream
¼ C. almond paste
½ tsp. ground nutmeg

Preheat oven to 350°. Pound chicken breast halves with a mallet to about ¼" thickness; season with salt and pepper to taste. In a shallow dish, combine egg and water. Place chopped almonds in a separate shallow dish. Dip chicken first into the egg mixture, letting any excess drip off, and then into the almonds, turning until well coated on both sides. Heat butter and oil in a large nonstick skillet over medium-high heat. Sauté chicken until browned, about 3 minutes on each side. Place chicken in a single layer in a lightly greased 9 x 13" baking dish; set aside. In the same skillet over medium-high heat, sauté mushrooms, onion slices and garlic until softened; spread over chicken. Heat heavy cream and almond paste in the same skillet over medium heat until thickened, about 5 minutes; stir in nutmeg. Pour sauce over chicken and mushrooms. Bake, uncovered, for 30 to 40 minutes or until chicken is cooked through and the juices run clear.

Candied Pineapple Chicken

Makes 4 to 6 servings

1½ tsp. extra-virgin olive oil
1 C. dry bread crumbs
1 T. flour
1½ tsp. dried oregano
1¼ tsp. salt, divided
1 tsp. pepper
4 to 6 boneless, skinless chicken breast halves
¾ C. brown sugar
2 T. prepared yellow mustard
¼ C. ketchup
1½ tsp. Worcestershire sauce
1½ tsp. soy sauce
2 T. minced onion
½ C. water
4 to 6 canned pineapple rings

Preheat oven to 350°. Heat oil in a large nonstick skillet over medium-high heat. In a shallow dish, combine bread crumbs, flour, oregano, 1 teaspoon salt and pepper; mix well. Dredge chicken breast halves in bread crumb mixture. Sauté chicken in skillet until browned, about 3 minutes on each side. Place chicken in a single layer in a lightly greased 9 x 13" baking dish. In a large saucepan over low heat, combine brown sugar, mustard, ketchup, Worcestershire sauce, soy sauce, onion, remaining ¼ teaspoon salt and water; bring to a boil. Pour sauce over chicken. Cover baking dish with aluminum foil. Bake, covered, for 45 minutes. Top each chicken breast half with one pineapple ring. Cover dish and return to oven for 10 to 15 minutes or until chicken is cooked through and the juices run clear.

Quick Peach Glazed Chicken

Makes 4 servings

4 boneless, skinless chicken breast halves
1 T. butter, melted
Salt and pepper to taste
⅔ C. peach preserves
1 T. spicy brown mustard
1 tsp. balsamic vinegar
Pinch of dried thyme

Preheat oven to 350°. Pound chicken breast halves with a mallet to about ¼" thickness. Place chicken in a single layer in a lightly greased 9 x 13" baking dish. Spread melted butter over chicken and sprinkle with salt and pepper. Bake, uncovered, for 15 minutes. Meanwhile, in a medium bowl, combine peach preserves, mustard, vinegar and thyme; mix well. Brush glaze over chicken and bake, uncovered, for an additional 15 to 25 minutes or until chicken is cooked through and the juices run clear.

Stuffed Garlic Cheese Chicken Rolls

Makes 4 servings

1 (8 oz.) pkg. cream cheese, softened
1 tsp. garlic powder
⅛ tsp. onion powder
⅛ tsp. seasoned salt
⅛ tsp. pepper
1 tsp. dried chives
4 boneless, skinless chicken breast halves
¼ C. butter, melted
1 C. dry bread crumbs
½ C. grated Parmesan cheese

Preheat oven to 350°. In a medium bowl, combine cream cheese, garlic powder, onion powder, seasoned salt, pepper and chives; mix well and set aside. Pound chicken breast halves with a mallet to about ¼" thickness. Place melted butter in a shallow dish. In a separate shallow dish, combine bread crumbs and Parmesan cheese. Dip chicken first into the butter, letting any excess drip off, and then into the bread crumb mixture, turning until well coated on both sides. Place ¼ of the cream cheese mixture in the center of each chicken breast half; roll up and secure with toothpicks. Place chicken rolls in a single layer in a lightly greased 9 x 13" baking dish; drizzle with any remaining melted butter. Bake, uncovered, for 35 to 40 minutes or until chicken is cooked through and the juices run clear.

Cordon Bleu Chicken Rolls

Makes 4 servings

4 boneless, skinless chicken breast halves
4 slices deli ham
1 C. shredded mozzarella cheese, divided
4 slices deli salami
1 egg, beaten well
1 C. dry bread crumbs
Garlic powder to taste
Salt and pepper to taste

Preheat oven to 350°. Pound chicken breast halves with a mallet to about ¼" thickness. Place one ham slice, 2 tablespoons cheese and one salami slice over each chicken breast half; roll up and secure with toothpicks. Place egg in a shallow dish and bread crumbs in a separate shallow dish. Dip chicken rolls first into the egg, letting any excess drip off, and then into the bread crumbs, turning until well coated. Place chicken rolls in a single layer in a lightly greased 9 x 13" baking dish; sprinkle with garlic powder, salt and pepper to taste. Bake, uncovered for 35 minutes. Sprinkle remaining ½ cup mozzarella cheese over chicken and bake, uncovered, for 5 minutes or until the cheese is melted and the chicken is cooked through.

Havarti Chicken with Shrimp

Makes 4 servings

1 (16 to 24 oz.) jar spaghetti sauce
½ lb. peeled cooked shrimp, tails removed
4 boneless, skinless chicken breast halves
Italian seasoning to taste
¼ lb. Havarti cheese, thinly sliced
4 strips bacon
4 tsp. prepared pesto sauce
Grated Parmesan cheese

Preheat oven to 350°. Pour spaghetti sauce into a 9 x 13" baking dish; add shrimp and toss until evenly coated. Pound chicken breast halves with a mallet to about ¼" thickness; rub evenly with Italian seasoning. Place a few slices of Havarti over each chicken breast; roll up and wrap one slice of bacon around each, securing with toothpicks. Place chicken rolls in a single layer over shrimp and sauce in dish. Top each roll with one teaspoon of pesto sauce and sprinkle with desired amount of Parmesan cheese. Bake, uncovered, for 35 to 45 minutes or until chicken is cooked through and the juices run clear.

Mozzarella Stick Chicken Rolls

Makes 4 servings

1 T. garlic powder
1 tsp. dried oregano
½ tsp. pepper
4 boneless, skinless chicken breast halves
4 mozzarella cheese sticks, unwrapped
1 C. frozen onion and bell pepper strips, divided
1 T. extra-virgin olive oil
1 (10.7 oz.) can cream of chicken soup

Preheat oven to 350°. In a small bowl, combine garlic powder, oregano and pepper; set aside. Pound chicken breast halves with a mallet to about ½" thickness; rub evenly with garlic powder mixture. Place one cheese stick over each chicken breast half and top each with ¼ cup of the frozen onions and bell peppers. Roll up chicken around cheese and vegetables, securing with toothpicks. Heat oil in a large nonstick skillet over medium-high heat. Sear chicken rolls in pan, turning until all surfaces are golden brown. Place chicken rolls in a single layer in a lightly greased 8" square baking dish. Pour soup over chicken. Bake, uncovered, for 35 to 45 minutes or until chicken is cooked through and the juices run clear.

Honey and Gouda Stuffed Chicken

Makes 4 servings

1 C. shredded smoked Gouda cheese
10 green olives, finely chopped
1 small clove garlic, minced
1 tsp. salt
4 T. honey, divided
6 to 8 green onions, minced
1 (10.7 oz.) can cream of chicken soup
1 (6.5 oz.) can mushrooms stems and pieces, drained
½ C. dry bread crumbs
4 boneless, skinless chicken breast halves
2 T. extra-virgin olive oil

Preheat oven to 375°. In a medium bowl, combine cheese, olives, garlic, salt, 3 tablespoons honey, green onions, soup, mushrooms and bread crumbs; mix well. Pound chicken breast halves with a mallet to about ½" thickness. Place ¼ of the cheese mixture in the center of each chicken breast half; roll up and secure with toothpicks. In a small bowl, combine remaining 1 tablespoon honey and oil; brush over chicken. Place chicken rolls in a single layer in a lightly greased 9 x 13" baking dish. Bake, uncovered, for 30 to 35 minutes or until chicken is cooked through and the juices run clear.

Pecan Stuffing Chicken Rolls

Makes 4 servings

4 boneless, skinless chicken breast halves
Salt and pepper to taste
1 (6 oz.) pkg. chicken-flavored stuffing mix
½ C. chopped pecans
2 T. butter
1 (10.7 oz.) can cream of mushroom soup

Preheat oven to 400°. Pound chicken breast halves with a mallet to about ¼" thickness. Sprinkle chicken on both sides with salt and pepper to taste. Prepare stuffing mix according to package directions. Meanwhile, sauté pecans in butter in a small skillet over medium-high heat until lightly toasted; stir into stuffing. Spoon about ½ cup of the stuffing mixture down the center of each chicken breast half; roll up and secure with toothpicks. Place chicken rolls in a single layer in a lightly greased 9 x 13" baking dish. Spoon soup over chicken and sprinkle with any remaining stuffing mixture. Bake, covered, for 25 to 30 minutes or until chicken is cooked through and the juices run clear.

Cajun Sausage Stuffed Chicken

Makes 4 servings

½ lb. smoked sausage, thinly sliced
½ lb. fresh button mushrooms
3 T. chopped green onions
1 small clove garlic, minced
5 T. blue cheese dressing, divided
4 boneless, skinless chicken breast halves
1 T. Cajun seasoning

Preheat oven to 375°. Brown sausage in a large nonstick skillet over medium-high heat. Once sausage begins to brown, stir in mushrooms; sauté for 5 minutes. Stir in green onions and garlic; sauté for 2 minutes. Transfer sausage, mushrooms, green onions and garlic to a food processor; add 1 tablespoon blue cheese dressing. Pulse until roughly chopped. Cut a slit sideways into each chicken breast half, making a pocket. Stuff a generous amount of the sausage mixture in the pocket in each chicken breast half, securing with toothpicks. Season both sides of each chicken piece with Cajun seasoning. Sauté chicken in the same skillet over medium-high heat until lightly browned, about 3 minutes on each side. Place stuffed chicken in a single layer in a lightly greased 9 x 13" baking dish. Spread remaining 4 tablespoons blue cheese dressing over chicken. Bake, uncovered, for 30 to 35 minutes or until chicken is cooked through and the juices run clear.

Feta and Spinach Stuffed Chicken

Makes 4 servings

½ C. mayonnaise
1 (10 oz.) pkg. frozen chopped spinach,
  thawed and drained
½ C. crumbled feta cheese
2 cloves garlic, minced
4 boneless, skinless chicken breast halves
4 strips bacon

Preheat oven to 375°. In a medium bowl, combine mayonnaise, spinach, feta cheese and garlic; mix well and set aside. Cut a slit sideways into each chicken breast half, making a pocket. Stuff a generous amount of the spinach mixture in the pocket in each chicken breast half. Wrap one slice of bacon around each stuffed chicken piece, securing with toothpicks if needed. Place stuffed chicken in a single layer in a lightly greased 9 x 13" baking dish. Bake, uncovered, for 30 to 35 minutes or until chicken is cooked through and the juices run clear.

Index

Chicken Out Your Dinner

Cubed, Sliced & Shredded

Sautéed & Fried

Grilled & Broiled

Baked